THE PEAK D

ON FOO⊥

by

Frank Rodgers

Photography by the author

ABOUT THIS BOOK

Many of the 31 walks in this new collection of walks visit some of the lesser-known places. Interesting features are pointed out with a brief reference to their history, thus adding to the pleasures of walking in this beautiful area. The walks are listed here in alphabetical order based upon the starting point in each case.

THE COUNTRY CODE

Guard against all risk of fire.

Fasten all gates.

Keep dogs under proper control.

Keep to the paths across farm land.

Avoid damaging fences, hedges and walls.

Leave no litter.

Safeguard water supplies.

Protect wild life, wild plants and trees.

Go carefully on country roads.

Respect the life of the countryside.

Published by Derbyshire Countryside Ltd.,

Lodge Lane, Derby, DE1 3HE.

Front cover: On Curbar Edge

Opposite above: on Mam Tor
Opposite below: Water-cum-Jolly

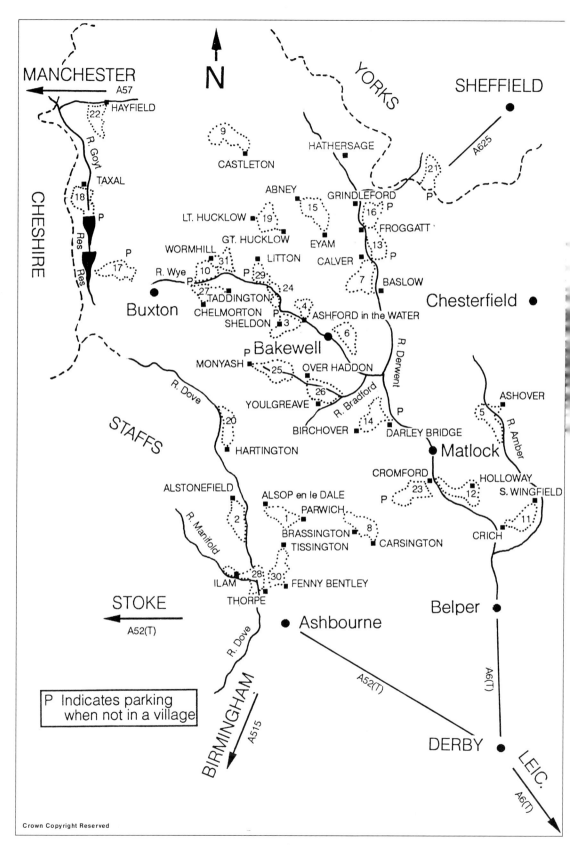

MANCHESTER

SHEFFIELD

YORKS

N

A57

HAYFIELD
22

CHESHIRE

R. Goyt

TAXAL
18
P

Res

Res
P
17

9
CASTLETON

HATHERSAGE

21
P

A625

ABNEY
15

GRINDLEFORD
P
16

FROGGATT

LT. HUCKLOW
19

GT. HUCKLOW

EYAM

13
P

WORMHILL
31
LITTON
CALVER

R. Wye
P
10
P
29
24
7
BASLOW

27
TADDINGTON
4

CHELMORTON
P
3
ASHFORD in the WATER

SHELDON

Buxton

6

P Bakewell

MONYASH
25
OVER HADDON

R. Derwent

Chesterfield

R. Dove

26

YOULGREAVE
R. Bradford
P

ASHOVER
5
R. Amber

STAFFS

20

BIRCHOVER
14
DARLEY BRIDGE

HARTINGTON

Matlock

ALSTONEFIELD

CROMFORD

HOLLOWAY
S. WINGFIELD

R. Manifold
2
ALSOP en le DALE
1
PARWICH
23
P
12
11

BRASSINGTON
8
TISSINGTON
CARSINGTON
CRICH

28
30
FENNY BENTLEY
ILAM
THORPE

STOKE

A52(T)

R. Dove

Ashbourne

Belper

A6(T)

P Indicates parking
when not in a village

BIRMINGHAM

A515

A52(T)

DERBY

LEIC.

A6(T)

Crown Copyright Reserved

2

CONTENTS

No. 1:
Alsop-en-le-Dale

Route: Alsop-en-le-Dale car park (Tissington Trail) – Alsop-en-le-Dale – Parwich – Bletch Brook – Tissington Trail – Car park

Distance: 5½ miles

Map: Outdoor Leisure Map O.S. 1:25,000 – The White Peak

Car park: Alsop-en-le-Dale (Tissington Trail)

The villages of Alsop-en-le-Dale and Parwich which are visited on this walk lie on a pleasant minor road which runs down a quiet valley from its junction with the A515 Ashbourne to Buxton road. This busy main road was crossed and recrossed by the railway – now the Tissington Trail – and its stations are now car parks very convenient for the famous dales of the River Dove only a mile or two away to the west. In great contrast to that popular area, the countryside to the east is not so well known, and much more gentle in its terrain. Nevertheless this walk, although short, is hilly enough to seem much longer! It drops steeply down to Alsop-en-le-Dale and then climbs the far hillside before descending gradually to Parwich. From there it crosses the valley again to return along the level stretch of the Tissington Trail.

Leave the car park by crossing the trail opposite its entrance and enter a field over a stile. Follow the wall downhill soon crossing a stile to the other side when Alsop-en-le-Dale is seen below among the trees. The well-kept fields sloping up the valley sides and neat enclosed woods have all the appearance of parkland and one fully expects to see a great house in the scene. The close-cropped grass indicates that this is sheep country, so be prepared for very narrow stiles!

In the valley bottom you join the lane and turn right. The attractive 17th century hall, once the home of the Alsops, may be glimpsed through the trees on the left facing the little church. In the churchyard you may be surprised to find that the church tower, which seen from the hill, you felt sure was Norman is a mere century old. It does, however, retain the Norman doorway from the previous building, with more Norman work inside. A little further along the road the Old Manor Farm is seen on the left, and at the last cottage on the left you leave the road by climbing a stile at the corner of the cottage garden.

Your route climbs in the direction of the electricity pole on the right to cross two stiles. Over the second one you turn right to pass a dew pond and enter a wood near the corner. The wind sighs among the tall trees on this hill top and the wood is loud with the raucous cries of rooks. Out of the wood you follow the wall to cross another stile and continue down the dip in the middle of the next field. Below you the fields flatten, and stiles can be seen in line with the spire of Parwich Church seen among the trees in the distance. The tree-crowned hill seen over to the left is Parwich Hill. As you cross the fields the house on the left is Peakway, and you cross its drive and drop down the open field to a stile in the corner on the right. Cross the next drive near its junction with the

4

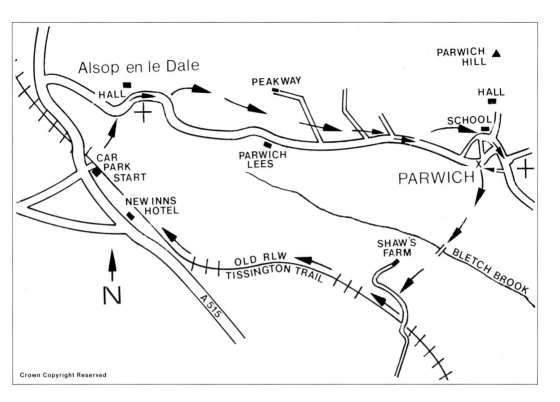

Alsop en le Dale

PARWICH HILL ▲

PEAKWAY

HALL

HALL

SCHOOL

CAR PARK START

PARWICH LEES

PARWICH

NEW INNS HOTEL

N

SHAW'S FARM

BLETCH BROOK

OLD RLW TISSINGTON TRAIL

A 515

Crown Copyright Reserved

road, and over a stile follow the hedge to join the road at a gate.

Continue along the road and where it dips cross a stile beside a gate on the left and climb a rough track to a stile. At this lower level hedges have replaced walls, still with the narrow limestone stiles, and you cross several small fields to come suddenly within site of Parwich. It presents a very pleasant picture, with the attractive school close by, the church surrounded by limestone cottages, and Parwich Hall on the lower slopes of Parwich Hill not far away on the left. Built in the mid 18th century, the hall has a brick façade which stands out above the white cottages without looking incongruous.

The path joins the road beside the school and, should you wish to give the village a miss, cross over and go forward to the place marked with an 'X' on the map. The church and village centre, however, are well worth a visit and for these turn left past the school. Like the one at Alsop-en-le-Dale, the church was rebuilt little over a century ago and retains parts of the Norman church it replaced, notably the west doorway with its tympanum carved with animals. From the churchyard turn left round cottages and within about 50 yards turn right beside the brook. Continue beside the brook along a narrow path to emerge on the road at point marked 'X', on the map mentioned previously.

Here you cross the brook (signpost Tissington) cross the stile seen up the hill, and aim towards another midway along the edge on the hilltop. The path follows the hedge on your right to a footbridge in the corner. Below lies the valley you crossed at Alsop-en-le-Dale, now much wider and having acquired a brook. Your route is clearly seen over the footbridge in the valley bottom where Bletch Brook tends to overflow and needs stepping stones too. From here the path goes straight up the hill to a stile and continues to join the farm road which serves Shaw's Farm seen over on the right. Turn left to cross the bridge over the Tissington Trail, turning left to join it and pass under the bridge.

The London and North Western Railway opened in 1899, was closed to passengers in 1954 and finally closed 10 years later. In the 1960s it was acquired by the Peak Park and turned into a trail. The walk back to the car park is easy and pleasant with limestone cuttings and high embankments, the latter giving extensive views across the valley you have traversed.

No. 2: Alstonefield

Route: Alstonefield – Stanshope – Hall Dale – Dovedale – Milldale – Alstonefield

Distance: 4½ miles

Map: Outdoor Leisure Map O.S. 1:25,000 – The White Peak

Car park: Alstonefield

This walk begins in the village of Alstonefield on the hills of Staffordshire and enters Derbyshire by crossing the River Dove in Dovedale, returning beside the river through Milldale. This beautiful area has been acclaimed by the famous, notably Izaak Walton and Charles Cotton who immortalised it in the 17th century classic *The Compleat Angler*. Milldale and Dovedale are very popular at summer weekends, but if you take this walk in early spring when not so busy you will be rewarded by the sight of great drifts of snowdrops, (if you don't mind the possibility of lingering snowdrifts!) A few weeks later the snowdrops are replaced by masses of daffodils. It may however, be muddy in the Dale Bottom and Hurt's Wood.

From the car park turn right and right again to the main road and then sharp left and left immediately along a narrow farm road. Where this turns sharp right go through a stile ahead and follow the wall side downhill. In the corner of the field turn right, and as you drop steeply and perhaps muddily beside the wall into Dale Bottom, think of the trains of heavily laden packhorses which once struggled up and down

this steep hillside, for this was a packhorse track between Alstonefield and Stanshope.

Beside the road is a pretty cottage, its lawns completely covered with snowdrops in spring, spilling out on to the roadside verges. They continue like snowdrifts beside the farm road opposite, (the packhorse track you still follow), and are now mixed with countless daffodils in bud. On the hilltop the track joins the main road at Stanshope where there are many more snowdrops, a bank of them fronting the old hall which looks down the meadows sloping to the head of Hall Dale. Here you turn left along a farm road (signpost Milldale) and at the corner of the second field on the right cross a stile (signpost Dovedale). Cross another stile close by on the left and turn down the field into Hall Dale.

This lovely dry dale deepens and narrows with Hurt's Wood on the right, and as it drops to the River Dove a superb view is revealed, with the towering limestone crags across Dovedale enclosing the scene. Cross the stile into Hurt's Wood, once carpeted with daffodils, but less so now with so many footpaths winding through it. More memories came flooding back at the footbridge over the river: of having tea in a small wooden tearoom here, the water being drawn from the river. Today there is not a trace left of this little building.

Cross the bridge and turn upstream past the Dove Holes, and then Ravens Tor on the opposite side. The valley widens as you approach Milldale where you cross Viator's Bridge, mentioned in the second part of *The Compleat Angler* written by Charles Cotton. This little packhorse bridge is sometimes referred to as The Wheelbarrow Bridge, so called from Viator's often quoted remark 'What's here, the

Crown Copyright Reserved

Opposite: tranquil Dovedale

Did this walk 4 July 2013. Very steep in parts but very pretty. Cool then warm. Had ice cream at Milldale and altered route back to

Below: snowdrops at Stanhope

Alstonefield. Mod / mile steep!!! climb back to Village Church. Went through Churchyard and into church.

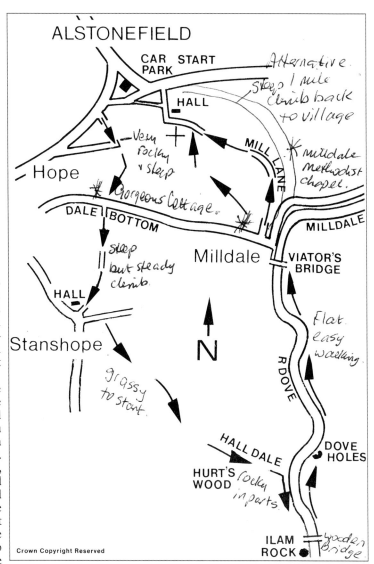

ALSTONEFIELD

CAR PARK — START

HALL

Alternative. Steep 1 mile climb back to village

Hope

Very rocky & steep

MILL LANE

Milldale Methodist chapel.

Gorgeous Cottage.

DALE BOTTOM

MILLDALE

Steep but steady climb.

Milldale

VIATOR'S BRIDGE

HALL

N

Flat. easy walking.

Stanshope

grassy to start.

R. DOVE

HALL DALE

HURT'S WOOD — rocky in parts.

DOVE HOLES

ILAM ROCK

wooden bridge

sign of a bridge? Do you use to travel with wheelbarrows in this county?'. The Old Millers Cottage close by and a grindstone lying in the mill-stream remind us of the corn mill from which this little hamlet took its name.

Cross the road into Mill Lane which curves round the hillside up to Alstonefield, but should you wish to cross the fields you will find a signpost within a short distance on the left. Narrow steps climb into a field, the path runs beside a wood before curving away from it and aiming towards a corner of the field. You then cross the next field diagonally and cross a stile in the corner and turn right up the open field to a gate to the right of the church now in sight, where you rejoin the road. You may, however, choose to stay on this ancient road, the road taken by Charles Cotton and Walton over 300 years ago while on their way to Beresford Hall, Cotton's home in Beresford Dale higher up the Dove. When the church came in sight, it drew forth another surprised comment from Viator, 'What have we here, a church? As I'm a honest man, a very pretty church!'

The church looks much the same as it would have done in Cotton's day and you should turn through the churchyard and look in the church if possible. Here is the Cotton family box pew, canopied and decorated with panels carved with grapes and flowers, where Cotton and Walton often sat. The church has retained its 17th century box pews, notable being those of the Beresford family with the name carved on the door. The church is mainly 16th century, but you will find evidence of the Norman and Saxon churches which preceded it.

Leave the churchyard by the main gate. The Elizabethan Manor House is seen on the right, and then *The George* on the left facing the green. Ahead is seen the main road, and here you turn left to bring the car park in sight.

7

The Wye Valley above Ashford-in-the-Water

Opposite below: Magpie Mine

No. 3: Ashford-in-the-Water

Route: Ashford - Magpie Mine - Sheldon - Great Shacklow Wood - Ashford

Distance: 5½ miles

Map: Outdoor Leisure Map O.S. 1:25,000 The White Peak

Car park: Fennel Street

Regular walkers in the central area of Derbyshire known as the White Peak cannot fail to have noticed the evidence left by the old lead miners. There are a number of paperback books on the history of the many lead mines there, and some knowledge of this ancient industry can add greatly to the pleasure of walking in this lovely area. One of the most important mines was the Magpie Mine near Sheldon, and this walk passes through the remains of the workings.

Whether or not you are interested in our industrial past, this is a very pleasant walk, climbing from Ashford-in-the-Water to Sheldon high above the River Wye, to return through Great Shacklow Wood and along the bank of the river. It should be mentioned that there is a stretch of a few hundred yards down the side of the wood which is very steep and rocky. Ashford is a delightful limestone village, situated, as its name implies, beside the river. Fennel Street, (car park) runs up from the river near the

church. Ancient funeral garlands, once carried at the funerals of maidens, hang in the church; relics found in only two other Derbyshire churches. Close by is an old tithe barn and the restored pump-house where the river is crossed by the well-known Sheepwash Bridge.

Go over the old packhorse bridge, noting its sheep enclosure, and cross the bypass to climb a short track to a gate. Through the gate continue past a farm to climb steadily round the hillside with extensive views up the valley. The path of your return route can be seen beside the river far below, and to the right walled fields climb to Fin Cop. The path passes a radio mast and follows the wall to a small gate into a road. Turn right and pass Arrock Plantation to the road in Kirkdale. Cross the road to a stile and make the short steep climb to the road above.

Turn right, and where the village of Sheldon comes in sight a sign on the left points along a rough road to the Magpie Mine, and soon the mine chimney comes into view. According to tradition, the mine is about 300 years old and has a fascinating history. Several lead veins intersect here, and a number of shafts were sunk under different ownership. When there was a break through into another mine there was trouble, efforts being made to smoke the other party out. A curse was placed on the mine when several miners were suffocated in 1833. As one approaches the main engine house and chimney, the blacksmith's shop is seen beside the gate to the left. This is now the Field Centre of the Peak District Historical Mines Society. The main shaft at the engine house is nearly 700 feet deep, and when it became uneconomical to pump out the

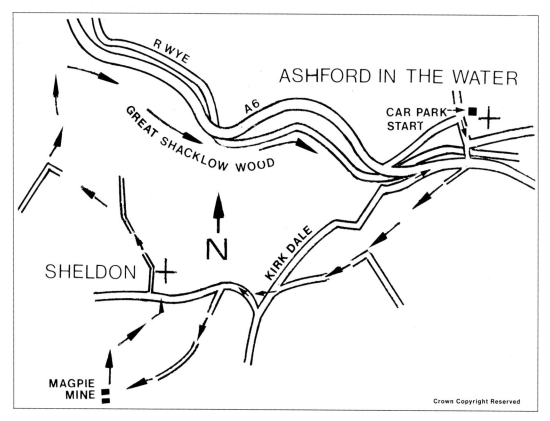

Crown Copyright Reserved

water, (the old enemy of lead miners) a sough was dug to drain it into the River Wye. You will pass the outlet in Great Shacklow Wood.

Pass the large chimney, (the 'jiggers' close by were used for riddling the ore) and go forward to a stile in the far corner of the mine area, continuing slightly left to the corner of the next field. Through the stile, turn right down the wall side, cross two small fields straight ahead and follow the side of a wall towards a barn seen ahead and continuing down to the road. Turn left into the village and then right to the church where the road becomes a cart track. In a little over a quarter of a mile cross a stile on the left, then another a short distance down to the right, to follow the wall on the left over several fields to enter a green lane which served lead mines here. Where this turns sharp left, cross the stile on the right and follow the wall to cross a stile in the next field. Here you follow the wall before aiming towards the edge of Great Shacklow Wood on a now worn path. The way down the woodside is steep and rocky, as already mentioned, and near the bottom you turn thankfully into the wood.

The path undulates along the steep hillside, and where it drops to the river the tail of the sough from the mine pours its clear waters into the Wye. Stand on the river bank and look at this small tunnel. The mine is over a mile away and 500 feet above the river. In 1873 the tunnel was started, aiming to meet the flooded mine shaft in a gradual climb. Eight years later a small pilot hole broke through into the shaft,

releasing pressurised water which chased the miners back down the long tunnel in the darkness. Derbyshire has many such soughs, some longer and others with branches to serve several mines, all testifying to the skill, courage and tenacity of the old miners. The ruptured ground seen above the tunnel was caused by the tunnel becoming blocked in 1966 and the water bursting out of the hillside.

Soon the path passes an old bone mill with two rusting water wheels, with close by a small water wheel. The latter was used to pump water up to Sheldon, beneath which village the sough had poured its waters down into the river! The path follows the river to the Sheldon road where a ruined bridge across the river no doubt carried the famous Ashford black marble to the now vanished mill. The marble came from Arrock Quarry which is passed on the right, and then the bypass is joined where you turn right to the Sheepwash Bridge.

9

No. 4: Ashford-in-the-Water

Route: Ashford – Monsal Head – Little Longstone – Ashford

Distance: 4 miles

Map: Outdoor Leisure Map O.S. 1:25,000 – The White Peak

Car park: Fennell Street

The second walk from this charming village; this one begins with a gentle climb up the slopes of Fin Cop in a lesser-known approach to Monsal Head. The path strikes the dale some distance from the famous view point with a sudden breathtaking view down into the depths of Monsal Dale. It should be mentioned that a short portion of the path running along the steep side of the dale to the Head is very narrow and should be taken with care. The return is through Little Longstone village and then down the fields back to Ashford.

About 50 yards up Fennell Street where the car park is situated a path strikes back on the left on a sharp right bend (signpost). This skirts new houses and where it enters a field go straight up the hill. Where a hedge comes into view on the right, aim towards the corner of the field where it ends on the left. Here is a stile where you enter a rough farm road and turn left. The road climbs steadily, zig-zagging around the fields which it serves, and where it enters the last field you follow the wall uphill to a gate and stile. The view ahead has been restricted by the sloping hill which terminates in Fin Cop, that great headland which towers over Monsal Dale. Looking backwards the view is wide and open with the hogsback of Longstone Edge filling the skyline on the left and the wooded valley of the Wye around Bakewell in the distance on the right. Cross the stile, turn right, enter a short farm road and cross two further stiles and you stand on the edge of the dale. In this superb view the diminutive Wye curves round the base of Fin Cop, and one can understand Iron Age men building their fort on the summit of this impregnable hill. Halfway down its slopes a natural rocky outcrop called Hobs House looks very much like a ruined castle. Across the valley, Brushfield Hough Farm is seen on the hilltop. Walk No. 24 passes through the farm, continuing along the hillside and dropping into the dale beyond the viaduct and returning beneath it beside the river. Away up the valley the grey houses of Cressbrook Village cling to the hillside.

The way along the edge of the dale is a broad green path towards the hotel at Monsal Head and where this ends at a field gate you continue with the wall on your right. This is the very narrow path along the steep side of the dale previously mentioned and one should be very careful. Far below, the railway route, now the Monsal Trail, is seen crossing the viaduct. The well-known beauty spot at Monsal Head has its refreshments and can be very busy. Here you cross

Opposite: the sheepwash bridge at Ashford-in-the-Water

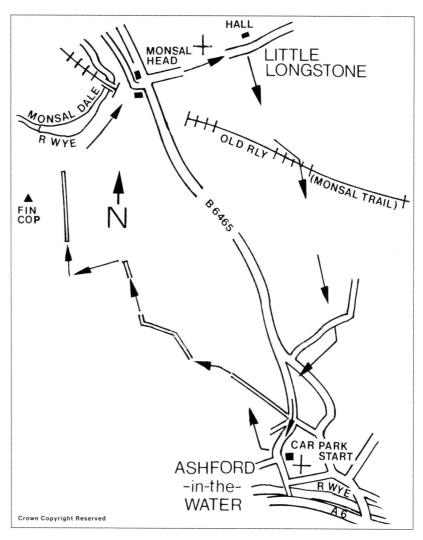

Crown Copyright Reserved

Below: the hills above Ashford

the road towards Little Longstone, passing the unusual and attractive little church and cottages. Just past the *Packhorse Inn* you have the choice of two stiles and two signposts close together! Here two footpaths meet and yours is the one on the right. As you proceed down a shallow valley a backward look shows the 17th century hall. Crossing several fields the path veers left beside a railway embankment and then crosses it. This is the Monsal Trail not far from the tunnel which comes out over the viaduct in the dale and the route you have been on from Monsal Head is the deviation to avoid the now closed tunnel.

The way ahead is straightforward, a clear path down a valley towards Ashford seen in the distance. You cross a road and follow the side of a wood and then a wall down to a barn in a dip. Here a stile gives access to an enclosed path which rises to a road. Cross over and cross a narrow field to another road where you turn left into Ashford. At the top of the hill the road continues down to the car park but should you wish to see the village turn left noting the stockinger's house on the left about halfway down.

Turn right at the bottom and go on to the church which has Norman remains and other interesting features mentioned in the previous walk. This charming corner makes a fitting end to a short but very pleasant walk.

11

No. 5: Ashover

Route: Ashover – Goss Hall – Overton Hall – Milltown – Ashover

Distance: 4½ miles

Map: Landranger Series O.S. Sheet No. 119

Car park: Ashover

Ashover, a quiet charming village off the beaten track, is the start of this walk. It covers ground not so well known, yet these upper reaches of the Amber Valley are lovely and full of interest. Ashover itself is well worth a protracted stroll, and as this walk is an easy one you should try to include it. This walk visits the church, climbs to Goss Hall, continues along a rough road to pass Overton Hall, and drops down to Milltown. The return route is along the hillside above the River Amber.

From the car park turn left to the church. At the churchyard gate the *Crispin Inn*, with its historical past set out on a large colourful board, faces the pretty, old school. Within the church is a finely carved Norman font made of lead. There are about 40 lead fonts in this country, yet, strangely in a county with a history of extensive lead mining, this is the only one in Derbyshire. That we should still have it is due to the foresight of the rector who buried it during the Civil War. The soldiers who smashed all the windows in the church would have almost certainly melted it down for making bullets. The church history shows early connections with the Babingtons of Dethick, the ill-fated Anthony being the last member of the family.

Turn right, round the tower, to a stile in a corner of the churchyard. The path passes the playing fields and enters a road at an old coach house with an attractive dormer dovecote. Turn right and pass Butts Church, originally built by Matlock's John Smedley after a difference of opinion with the vicar of Ashover. At a dip in the road turn left through a stile and go forward along the flat beside the stream. Here was the terminus of the Ashover Light Railway which ran down the valley and then turned up to Clay Cross. Opened in 1925, it ran for only 34 years, and you will see slight evidence of it during this walk. Continue to the end of the open track, ignoring bridges over the River Amber, and then cross the river over a footbridge made of a single block of stone.

Follow the deep gully on your left, pass through a gap in the wall and go forward to a stile beside a gate. Through the stile turn right and follow the wall to pass through two stiles close together. Go straight up the field past Goss Hall to enter a lane and turn left. This goes on past Overton Hall, and when the hall comes in sight at a road junction, note a path on the right paved with stone slabs. This is obviously an ancient way and you will see more of this later.

Next you pass Overton Hall, the Derbyshire home of Sir Joseph Banks the famous naturalist who accompanied Captain Cook on his first journey round the world, a voyage which nearly ended on the Great Barrier Reef. This valley seems as remote now as it probably was in the 1700s and the unmade road little changed from when Banks wandered round its woods and hills. No doubt he would climb to Cocking Tor, a gritstone crag high above on a wooded ridge, its lower slopes littered with the workings of old lead mines.

At a sharp right bend, where the houses of Milltown come into sight, leave the road and go forward to a footpath sign. Follow the wall and drop down a few steps into a dip then turn right to emerge beside the *Miners Arms*. Note the stone trough and

Opposite: the Crispin Inn at Ashover

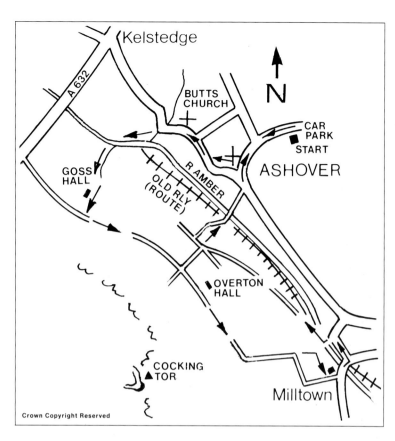

Kelstedge

A 632

BUTTS CHURCH

N

CAR PARK START

ASHOVER

GOSS HALL

R AMBER

OLD RLY (ROUTE)

OVERTON HALL

COCKING TOR

Milltown

Crown Copyright Reserved

Below: remains of the clapper bridge at Milltown

mounting steps carved from one block of stone, an unusual feature. Turn left to the river bridge, unknowingly crossing the route of the railway, and turn left. On the left the remains of a wide clapper bridge lie in the Amber, and as they point towards the road in front of the *Miners Arms*, it would seem that this was the route of the old road. Continue beside the river and where the road turns sharp right, leave it to cross the river into a quarry yard. Turn right to pass a few cottages.

The open lane climbs steadily up the valley side with Ashover coming into view. Across the valley two cottages stand alone. The one on the right, with a modern addition, was built in 1676 and was the home of Leonard Wheatcroft, poet, tailor, parish clerk and schoolmaster, whose diary, published in 1900, gives much information about Ashover in the 1700s. Where the lane reaches the hilltop it is crossed by an enclosed path, one wall being made of vertical stone slabs, a feature seen at a few other places in the county. Through a stile in these you traverse the open field on a stone causeway ('casey' in Derbyshire). This is a continuation of the one mentioned earlier and, as it comes from the lead mines below Cocking Tor, one wonders if it was the route through Ashover to the smelting cupola at Stone Edge about three miles up the valley.

The path drops into a sunken track, but before reaching the river look for a mounting block on the right, an odd feature in a lonely spot. Perhaps the

answer is in the railway mentioned earlier, for it crossed the track here, its raised route seen left and right along the valley. Old maps show a 'halt' and maybe folk from outlying farms were met here with horses. Such little features add interest to these walks, and still wondering you cross the Amber and climb the track to emerge beside the *Red Lion* where a left turn brings Ashover Church in sight.

No. 6: Bakewell

Route: Bakewell – Ball Cross – Carlton Pastures – Manners Wood – Old Coach Road – Monsal Trail – Bakewell

Distance: 5 miles

Map: Outdoor Leisure Map O.S. 1:25,000 – The White Peak

Car park: Bakewell Market Area (Full Monday Markets)

After the first three-quarters of a mile, part of which climbs steeply through Manners Wood, there is a level stretch over Carlton Pastures before returning in an easy fall back to Bakewell. There are no striking features (unless of course you look round Bakewell), but the route follows a packhorse track, possible prehistoric trackways, the old coach road between Rowsley and Bakewell and then the Monsal Trail. The landscape is very pleasant parkland created by the Dukes of Devonshire and Rutland, and although quite close to Chatsworth House and Haddon Hall neither house is seen.

From the 17th century Market Hall in Bakewell, turn right along Bridge Street to the fine 13th century bridge over the Wye and continue up towards the old station. The railway route is now the Monsal Trail, but you go forward to fork right up a rough track (signpost to Ball Cross). This is an ancient packhorse track crossing the hill between the Derwent and the Wye, and it zig-zags steeply up through the wood to emerge on a sharp road bend at Ball Cross. You do not use the road, but immediately leave it by crossing a stile beside a gate on the right (signpost to Rowsley) on to a rough road. Through a gate the track is open across Carlton Pastures, and may possibly have been a prehistoric ridge trackway, for in the field on the right can be seen a flat-topped mound, identified as a small Iron Age Fort.

The track climbs round a plantation on a hill, and from here can be seen its green route across the open meadows and you are now in Chatsworth Park. It passes to the left of a group of trees, and a stile can be seen beside a sheet of water. Here a footpath from Chatsworth to Bakewell crosses and we follow the sign pointing to Rowsley. The way is over open fields with no path, but over on the right Manners Wood closes the view and away in the distance can be seen the edge of the wood jutting out squarely into the field.

This is your line, and just past the point of the wood a stile is found. Here is a fine vantage point, looking across an open valley to New Piece Wood with Russian Cottage seen on the right, an obviously man-made landscape. Over the stile, follow the wall to a corner to bear left on a well defined path through

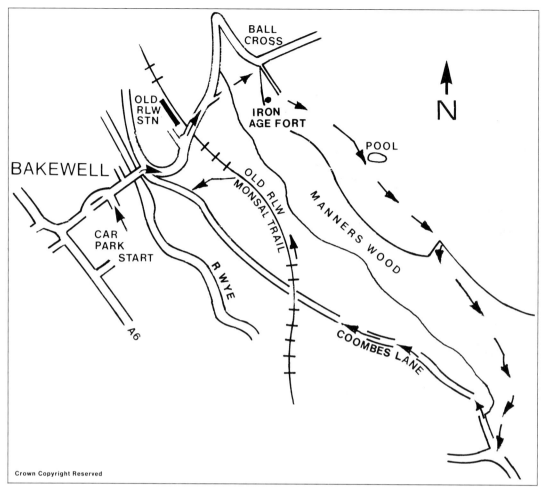

Crown Copyright Reserved

sparse trees. Where it passes through an open gateway it turns left, but go forward a few steps to admire the view into the Wye Valley with Bakewell far on the right. Here is a totally different scene from the parkland view just left on the other side of the hill.

Your route enters the wood between huge bracken, dropping steadily downhill and emerging at a junction with a rough road. This comes over the hill from Rowsley on the left to drop down to Bakewell on the right. Until the turnpike road was cut up the Wye Valley in the 1800s past Haddon Hall, this was the main road between these two places, and it may be that the rough road seen opposite was the way to the Hall. The way is down Coombes Lane to the right, and treading its rough track, probably no better now than when coaches rumbled down it and strained up it, one wonders at the difficulty of travel in those days.

You may continue on to Bakewell and the river bridge, or deviate a little as follows, giving pleasant views of the town. After passing under the railway bridge, turn right onto the Monsal Trail, leaving it by climbing onto the next railway bridge and dropping down to rejoin Coombes Lane and so into Bakewell.

Opposite: the Wye Valley

Below: in Manners Wood

15

No. 7:
Calver Bridge

Route: Calver Bridge – Bubnell – Baslow Bridge – Bank Wood – Bramley Wood – Calver – Calver Bridge

Distance: 5½ miles and 3 miles

Map: Outdoor Leisure Map O.S. 1:25,000 – The White Peak

Car park: Calver Bridge

The old bridge over the River Derwent which gives the name to Calver Bridge stands close by the new concrete span and here, opposite the craft centre and tearooms, a portion of the old road has parking for a few cars. This walk follows the river valley down to Baslow and then climbs the hills westwards. The return is over the hills through two miles of woodlands, the last half mile along a ridge with extensive views. The accompanying map shows a shorter walk passing Bramley Farm indicated X-X.

From the concrete bridge take the path along the river bank. The path becomes an open track which veers away from the river to turn round the foot of a wooded hill. Where this bends right you go straight ahead across an open field to a gate where a stile on the left gives access to a road. If you are taking the shorter walk you turn right up past Bramley Farm along a very pleasant lane, an old packhorse route with views into the green bowl of Bramley Dale. At the top of the hill you turn right through a gate (signpost) and join the longer walk.

For the longer walk you turn left on the road (X on the map) into Bubnell, a very quiet part of Baslow

where houses on the right include the fine 17th century hall, and old and new houses of Baslow line the bank across the river. The long weir points to the old corn mill across the water, now well looked after but minus its water-wheel. A little further on the narrow bridge, which replaced a wooden one in 1603, crosses the river at Bridge End in Baslow. The view downstream includes the church and the later bridge which put this fine old structure into semi-retirement. The church is well worth a visit and you will notice the tiny toll house across the bridge where a toll of 6/8d was charged for every pair of millstones carried across.

Returning over the bridge, cross the road to a stile between two houses where an enclosed path leads into the fields. Follow the wall on your right and where the wall turns right in the fourth field aim towards the top right corner. From this hilltop extensive views across the Derwent Valley include Baslow on the edge of Chatsworth Park backed by the high ridges of Baslow and Gardom's Edges. Continue beside the wall and in the third field bear left across to a gate and stile on a road.

Turn right and where two gateways face each other across the road in a dip, cross over the stile on the right. Climbing the steep field beside a wood, you enter it over a fence stile. This is Bank Wood and you have all the pleasures of walking beneath trees with various wildlife and, in this case, bluebells and rhododendrons if in season. Following the wall side the path climbs to its highest point and here you cross a stile and continue beside it to a road.

Here is the meeting with the shorter walk and you cross the road to a gate and enter Bramley Wood to follow its boundary wall. The path rises along a ridge with views down through the trees to old mine workings in the valley below and soon the views become wider as you pass through masses of rhodo-dendrons. This is a short but fine ridge walk where, if

Crown Copyright Reserved

Opposite: footpath above Calver

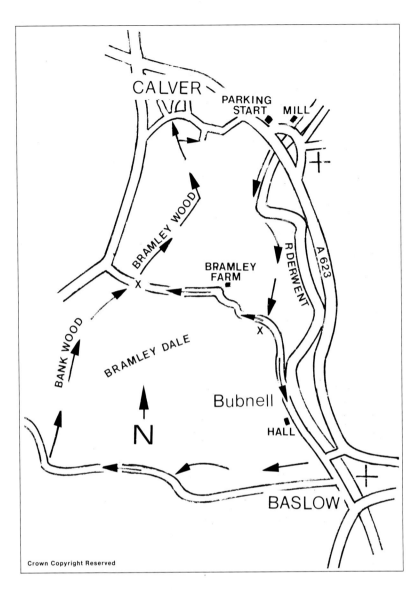

Below: the toll house on the bridge at Baslow

the day is clear, you may discern the fountain in Chatsworth Park way down the Derwent Valley. Where the ridge ends overlooking Calver there are extensive views up the valley with the dark gritstone edges of Curbar and Froggatt, while to the left the grey cottages of Eyam cling to Sir William Hill above Middleton Dale. Walks Numbers 13 and 16 go along the Curbar and Froggatt Edges, and Sir William Hill is crossed in Walk No. 15 from Eyam.

The end of the ridge is crowned by a clump of windswept trees where the map indicates a disused reservoir which supplied water to Calver but no evidence of this remains except disrupted ground. Here the path turns sharp left and twists steeply downhill to follow a wall and pass between cottages into the main street. Here you turn right and right again at an old water supply which may once have been the village cross. This quiet street is an old packhorse route down to the river crossing continu-

ing up through the Gap on Curbar Edge seen on the skyline. The street bears left to the main road and so back to the car park.

17

Old Carsington Pastures

No. 8: Carsington

**Route: Carsington – Brassington – Longcliffe –
High Peak Trail – Carsington**

Distance: 5½ miles

**Map: Outdoor Leisure Map O.S.
1:25,000 – The White Peak**

With the building of the new reservoir at Carsington, the A5035 which twisted through the village now slips by on a new by-pass to the south. Carsington is now a much quieter place and an ideal spot from which to start this walk. It climbs over Carsington Pasture to the village of Brassington, continues on to Longcliffe to join the High Peak Trail, and returns over the Pastures to make a very steep but short descent into Carsington.

The little church of St. Margaret has remains of the early 14th century and a sundial with the inscription 'Re-edified 1648', while the church registers record that the yew tree nearby was planted 100 years earlier. Opposite the church the stump of a Saxon Cross has been set on the little green, and close by the *Miners' Arms* reminds one that Carsington was a lead-mining village.

Leaving the churchyard turn right, and where the road turns sharp left continue forward past Townend Cottage. Miners Lane on the right was the route of the lead miners to the mines on Carsington Pasture,

and the steep hillside above is the return into the village already mentioned. At the last building the road becomes a track with a gate and stile (signposted to Brassington). For the next mile the track climbs steadily to Carsington Pasture, and where it bends left round two concrete-covered mine shafts you leave it to go straight ahead up a footpath. Here the ground is completely disrupted by hillocks and hollows of the lead mines, and it is not advisable to venture into the hollows as they may be covered mine shafts.

Pause and look back down the valley. In the distance is the valley of Scow Brook, soon to be flooded by the new reservoir. But up here you are in the past, for hereabouts you have passed over the Roman road which ran from Derby to Buxton, and there was a settlement in the valley near Carsington. On the hilltop pass through a gap in the wall on the left and through another close by in the wall on the right. The route goes down the open field to the left of a barn, and a stile is found in the left corner of a square field which leads to a lane.

Cross the stile opposite and follow the cart track round the hillside. Near the top leave the track for a path which forks left, and suddenly at the top a fine view of Brassington is seen across the valley. The path snakes down between more mine workings to a wall where a right turn is made beside it to a stile. Through this follow the wall to another stile and over this cross two fields in the direction of the church to enter the village through a farmyard.

Cross the road, and if you wonder about the oddly

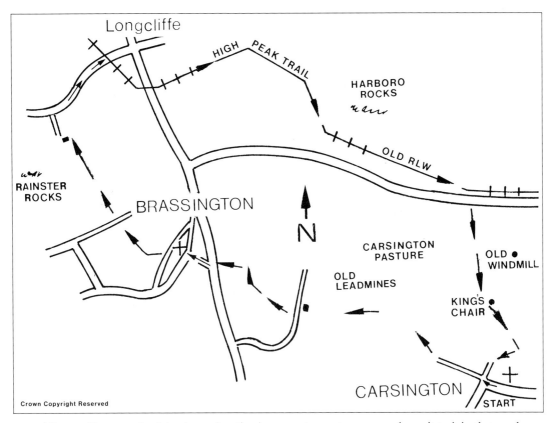

Longcliffe

HIGH PEAK TRAIL

HARBORO ROCKS

OLD RLW

RAINSTER ROCKS

BRASSINGTON

N

CARSINGTON PASTURE

OLD LEADMINES

OLD WINDMILL

KING'S CHAIR

CARSINGTON

START

Crown Copyright Reserved

named Dragon House on the right, the explanation is that it was once a public house. At the top of the road there is another *Miner's Arms* for Brassington was also a lead-mining village. Here the route goes through the churchyard across the road, where there are several interesting tombstones, the oldest dating from 1695. This paves the path and you cross it to enter the Norman doorway of the porch for one should have a look at this lovely old church. Outside again, turn round the tower to a stile at the top corner of the churchyard. Turn left down the lane to a small chapel, cross a stile opposite and climb obliquely left between outcrops of limestone when the path becomes clear.

Soon the little-known Rainster Rocks are seen on the left and when a farm comes into view ahead stiles will be found in line with it. The path closely passes round the right of the buildings to join a farm road where a right turn is made to the road. Turn right and in a quarter of a mile pass under the High Peak Trail to turn right into the site of the station at Longcliffe, and on to the trail. The next two miles are easy walking, giving extensive views over the surrounding hills. The Cromford and High Peak Mineral Railway was built in 1825, one of the first in England, and ran for 33 miles over the limestone dome of Derbyshire, linking Cromford Canal with that at Whaley Bridge. Soon the well-known Harboro Rocks are passed (you may leave the trail through a stile to explore the interesting features there) and where the trail comes close to a road at the

entrance to a quarry, leave it to join that road.

Turn right for about fifty yards and cross the road to a stepstile. The remains of a tower mill in the field on the left is an uncommon sight in the Peak District where storable water power was more readily available. The path follows the wall for about a mile, again climbing over Carsington Pasture but now on the eastern side. Note the King's Chair on the left, a limestone curiosity for which there seems no recorded reason for the name. When the wall ends at a wood turn right and slant away from it down the hillside. Aim for the nearest house in the village when a small black door will be found to the left of it bearing the words 'Public Footpath', and through it go down garden steps into the village.

The ruined windmill

19

The Ridge seen from Mam Tor

No. 9: Castleton

Route: Castleton – Mam Tor – Hollins Cross – Castleton

Distance: 4½ miles

Map: Outdoor Leisure Map O.S. 1:25,000 – The Dark Peak

Car park: Castleton

Dramatic scenery and historical associations abound around Castleton and in this walk you climb to the summit of Mam Tor where you stand on the site of an Iron Age fort and enjoy some of the finest panoramic views in the country. The path runs along the ridge eastwards and at Hollins Cross, the lowest

point on the ridge, you leave it to return to Castleton.

From the car park turn right along the main road to find a footpath between the villas (signpost). From the top of the few steps here a backward look gives a good view of Peak Cavern with the remains of the castle perched on its edge. The path enters a field where you bear left to a stile and then follow a narrow wood which shades a stream, Odin Sitch. Over on the left can be seen the entrance to the Winnats, and between that and Mam Tor is Treak Cliff with the entrance to Treak Cliff Cavern on its slopes.

Where you leave the trees you can see almost the whole of your route and the dark mass of Mam Tor ahead looks daunting but the effort is well worth while. The path bears away left to a farm, crosses the farm road in front of the house and climbs between a building and a steam. The path is clear, winding over

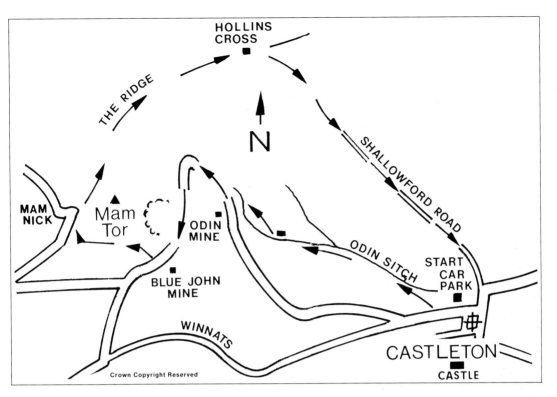

Crown Copyright Reserved

the residue which has slipped from the face of Mam Tor and the tailings from a lead mine fenced in here. Where you cross a stream, the Odin Mine is seen across the road. The earliest record of the mine, which looks like a natural cave, dates from 1280, but the name suggests that it was worked by the Danes. You are now standing on debris from the mine and the remains of the stone crusher close by have been dated as 1823.

Climb to the road and turn right where a notice board gives details of why the road is closed to traffic. The history of the Mam Tor landslide goes back an estimated 3,000 years, and to see the effect it has had on the road in recent years you follow it to the foot of the tor. Here you climb over the tortured roadway where the strata of many repairs through the years tells its own story. When you reach the stable road the entrance to the Blue John Cavern is seen on the left and then on the next left bend you cross a stile on the right.

The path climbs beside a wall and emerges in the road below Mam Nick, then leaves it in a few yards to cross a stile on the right, where broad new steps climb to the summit of Mam Tor. Today this once almost impregnable Iron Age fort is worn smooth by countless feet and one can see why it was chosen by those prehistoric folk. Across the Vale of Edale to the north lies the dark skyline of Kinder Scout and if the day is clear you can pick out the line of the Pennine Way worn smooth where it begins – or ends – in Edale village. To the south Castleton nestles in Hope Valley and the deep gorge of the Winnats is curiously diminished when seen from here.

To the east the ridge ends at Lose Hill and this is your route but you leave it where the ridge is lowest and before it climbs to Back Tor. This point is Hollins Cross where an ancient route between Edale and Castleton crosses. Standing on this exposed spot and looking down the steep hillsides to these lonely villages, imagine the trail of women and girls who once walked from Castleton to work in the mill at Edale. Even more remarkable is that until Edale had its own chapel, funeral cortèges used this path for burials in Castleton churchyard!

From Hollins Cross take the left well-worn path towards Castleton. This becomes enclosed by hawthorns, joins a farm road and then continues into Castleton where a right turn takes you back to the car park.

Subsidence on the road below Mam Tor

Castle Rock, Chee Dale

No. 10: Chee Dale

Route: Wye Dale car park – Chee Dale – Wormhill – Flag Dale (head) – Meadow – Chee Dale – Car park

Distance: 6½ miles

Map: Outdoor Leisure Map O.S. 1:25,000 – The White Peak

Car park: Wye Dale car park

Chee Dale, where the delightful River Wye is hemmed in by high crags, is probably the finest limestone gorge in Derbyshire. Like so much of the county's best scenery, it can only be visited on foot. In two places the path enters the river on stepping stones beneath overhanging cliffs, and in others climbs steeply on natural rocky steps. From the dale, your route climbs to the village of Wormhill and crosses the hills before dropping to the river again near a footbridge crossed earlier.

From Wye Dale car park, which lies between the river and the A6 at the bottom of Topley Pike, you can go along the rough road beside the river to Blackwell Mill. (Walk No. 27 also covers this section). Only the broken weir gives evidence of the mill which stood at this junction with Great Rocks Dale. Here a footbridge crosses the river to a row of cottages with a lovely view down the river, your route today. Impressive crags close in as you pass beneath a railway bridge (which now carries the Monsal Trail) the aptly named Castle Rock towering high above.

Lower down the dale the path resorts to stepping stones where the river has undercut the cliff, and you cross a footbridge and climb steeply to avoid a narrow gorge where a path is impossible. Here a high viaduct crosses the dale, for in 1863 a railway was built along this portion of the Wye Valley, a remarkable feat of engineering, and at this point, where the river makes a sharp turn, it emerged from a tunnel and crossed this very short viaduct before plunging into another tunnel. Passengers had a sudden brief view of the ravine before it was blacked out again, rather like the almost instantaneous click of a camera shutter!

Until the closure of the line about 20 years ago the deep silences here were suddenly shattered by the roar of an express, but today the silence is complete except for the birds and the river gurgling over its rocky bed. The path passes beneath the viaduct, crosses the river again and follows more steps beneath overhanging rock. Soon the 300 feet high crag of Chee Tor is passed, and the path climbs tortuously over a rocky bluff and drops to where Flag Dale with its underground stream joins the Wye.

Here too Wormhill Springs emerge from the rocks, and shortly after crossing these you leave the riverside path and fork left up the hillside. Where the path joins a wider one turn left up to the road, turning left into Wormhill village. To visit the church, turn right at the first junction to find one of the most secluded and unspoilt corners of the county. The church spire is very unusual, unique in Derbyshire, and although only dating from 1864 it stands on a base 700 years old. The churchyard merges into the grounds of the hall, views of which may have been noticed from the road.

Back on the main road you pass a memorial to 'James Brindley Civil Engineer, born in this parish A.D. 1716' who as a boy worked at the Old Manor Farm. Famous as the pioneer of canal construction, it is odd that he originated in countryside where canals were a practical impossibility. Pass the village stocks close by and continue up the road to turn into that same farm drive just past a telephone kiosk on the left (signpost). Go through the farmyard and bear left to go through the left one of two field gates, to follow the track beside the wall on the right.

In the third field you drop into a dip and join an enclosed field track which joins a good road with Tunstead, Brindley's birthplace, a short distance on the right. Here you turn left, cross the head of Flag Dale mentioned earlier and turn left at a junction. This quiet lane – it goes only to Mosley Farm –

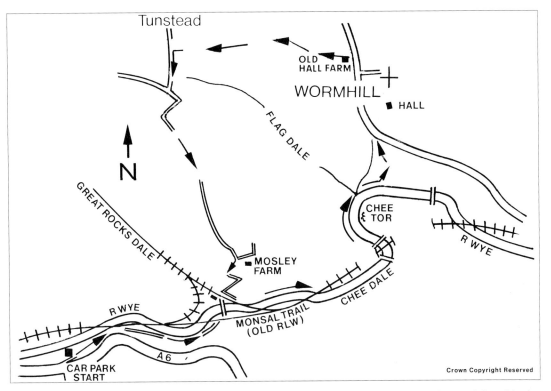

crosses the hills interlaced with white walls enclosing fields of peaceful sheep. Centuries ago they were heavily wooded and it is recorded that rents were once paid in wolves' heads.

Away on the right are seen glimpses of huge quarries in Great Rocks Dale and over on the left the abandoned limeworks on the slopes above Millers Dale. Where the lane dips and turns left to Mosley Farm go straight ahead and cross a stile into the fields. The path zig-zags beside the wall down into Chee Dale, revealing superb views. Turning right beneath a railway bridge, you can descend to the river and your outward route, turning right to the footbridge and back to the car park.

Brindley's Well,
Wormhill

23

Crich Market Place

No. 11: Crich

Route: Crich – Wingfield Park – Wingfield Manor – South Wingfield – Crich

Distance: 5 miles

Map: Outdoor Leisure Map O.S. 1:25,000 The White Peak

Car park: Crich Market Place

For nearly 200 years a tower has stood on the hilltop at Crich, indicating from far and wide the location of this quarry village above the Derwent Valley. Despite the popularity of the National Tramway Museum in the quarry below the present Crich Stand, the area of hills and dales east of the village is little walked, although there are numerous footpaths and bridleways and much of interest there. From Crich this walk goes over the hill to the Amber Valley with an unusual close look at Wingfield Manor, and returns over the fields from South Wingfield village.

The Market Place in Crich has a row of four stone troughs, dating from the days of the old markets, or maybe even from the days of the packhorses which once crossed these hills. A few yards down the road to Bull Bridge the long windows in a stockinger's house indicate this one-time cottage industry, and the quarry activities had connections with George Stephenson,

School Lane, on the bottom side of the Market Place, is your route. Just past the school a small gate leads into a field, and you continue down two small fields to cross a stile into a lane. Turn left to a gate where the lane ends. There is nothing here now to show that you stand on the route of an old railway built about 200 years ago to carry limestone from Hilts Quarry down to the kilns at Bull Bridge beside the River Amber. What must have caused excitement in the early 19th century was Brunton's locomotive which was propelled by two grasshopper-type legs fixed either side of the engine which

'walked' it along at a modest two and a half miles an hour!

Pass through a stile beside a gate (the left one of two here) and continue beside the hedge on your right for about 200 yards. Through a stile follow the hedge on your right and where this ends aim towards the corner of a hedge in line with a white house. Continue down this hedge-side along the next field, and at the bottom cross a stile and turn right to the road. This is Dimple Lane, and the large building seen up the road was once a hat factory and is now two private dwellings. The railway mentioned previously passed between the factory and the white house and beneath the road, and there are indications of a railway yard across the road from where we stand.

Turn left down the road and in a few hundred yards turn left up a rough lane beside a few houses. Opposite the last house a stile is found on the right. Over the stile, climb up two fields, towards the bottom corner of a wood. The village seen across the valley is Fritchley. Enter the wood through a stile and follow the path obliquely left to the far corner, emerging on to a rough track beside a gate on the left. Turn through a stile beside it and follow the track which curves round the hillside. Note the ruined tower mill over on the right.

Where your open track crosses a walled bridle way you can see Wingfield Manor in the distance but turn right down the bridle way to join the road at Wingfield Park and continue forward to its junction with Park Lane. Turn left to the few houses, including a converted cotton mill, and leave the road by turning through a stile beside the garden of the first house on the right. Follow the hedge on your left, and at the top of the hill the ruins of Wingfield Manor come in sight. The path joins a cart track, and where this turns into a farmyard pass through a gate straight ahead.

Here is an impressive but now unused gateway into the Manor. This gaunt pile on its hilltop site dates from the 15th century, and has its place in history as the prison of Mary Queen of Scots (three

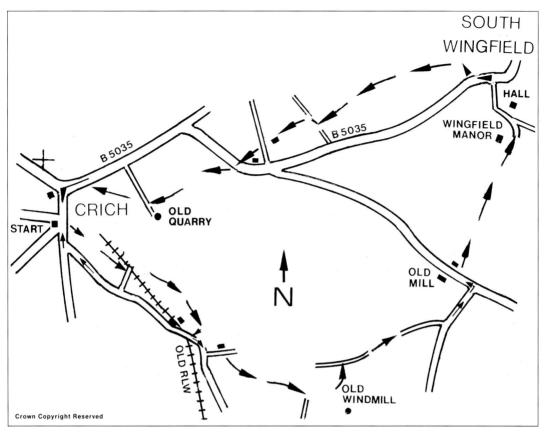

Crown Copyright Reserved

times) and was later under seige in the Civil War. Your way goes down a green track to curve left into a valley with the Hall seen across the brook, and climbs to the road at South Wingfield.

Turn left down to a bridge, and just before it cross a stile beside a gateway on the right. Follow the hedge to another stile and over it bear left past an electricity pole to cross a brook and stile. Bear right a few yards and cross a stile beside a gate. Turn left and continue beside the hedge for three long fields. Through the last stile cross two fields through stiles in line with an electricity pole and then pass this to the wall on the far side of the field. Turn right through a gateway and in about 50 yards a stile is found in the hedge.

Below: the old hat factory in Dimple Lane. Right: Wingfield Manor

Through the stile, cross a small field to a gateway; follow the wall and then cross it to continue along the opposite side to pass a farm and climb to a rough road. Turn left a short distance to a stile on the right, cross two small fields to the left of electricity poles and join the main road. Cross over to a stile beside a gate (ignoring one on the left) and following the hedge on your right for five fields, fork left down to a brook. Through a gateway here you climb to a new road which serves a quarry.

Crossing straight over to a stile you cross two fields in the direction of the spire of Crich Church and emerge in a road. The village lies to the left, and a left turn at the Cross takes you back to the Market Place.

Holloway Village

No. 12: Cromford

Route: Cromford – Lea Bridge – Holloway – Lea Hurst – Gregory Tunnel – Cromford Canal – Cromford

Distance: 6 miles

Map: Outdoor Leisure Map O.S. 1:25,000 The White Peak

Car park: Cromford Canal Wharf

There are numerous fascinating walks which can begin at Cromford, for the area is one of great beauty and full of interest. The restored Cromford Canal wharf is close by Sir Richard Arkwright's mill, open to the public, and near by are the church and Willersley Castle, both of which he also built. There is a fine car park at the canal wharf, and from there you go down the far hillside of the Derwent Valley to Lea Bridge, climb high above Holloway, and return past Lea Hurst, former home of Florence Nightingale, and so along the canal back to Cromford.

Turn right outside the car park to the river bridge. Here is an 18th century fishing temple, together with the remains of a 15th century bridge chapel, one of only seven still standing in the country. It is contemporary with the packhorse bridge, on the down-river side of the present bridge, which has been widened.

The curious inscription carved on the parapet commemorates the leaping of the parapet by a horse ridden by Benjamin Haywood of Bridge House nearby. Both landed safely in the river, the rider still seated!

Follow the road beside the river to find a stile on the left just past the railway bridge (signpost Lea and Dethick). Note the attractive French chateau-type Cromford Station on the left. Climb the worn path beside a wood and leave it to enter the wood along an avenue cut through the trees. At the end of the wood cross a stile beside a gate and follow the hedge to an open gateway. The green track bears left round the brow of the hill with extensive views along the valley. The corner of a wood seen ahead is your route, and you reach it by a stile down on the left and then you aim for a gate into a road.

Turn left past the wood and on a sharp left bend leave the road to pass through an open gateway on the right into a 'green' lane which passes in front of a cottage. Ahead is Bow Wood and the green track through it is delightful, emerging on the road at Lea Bridge. Turn left over the brook and left again between the buildings of John Smedley's mill, home of the famous knitting and spinning wares. The original mill was built by Peter Nightingale whose father built Lea Hurst not far away. The present mill was built by John Smedley, whose son John's hydropathic fervour developed the Matlocks into a spa.

Continue past the mill ponds, the original power for the mill, and then past a curious mound, residue

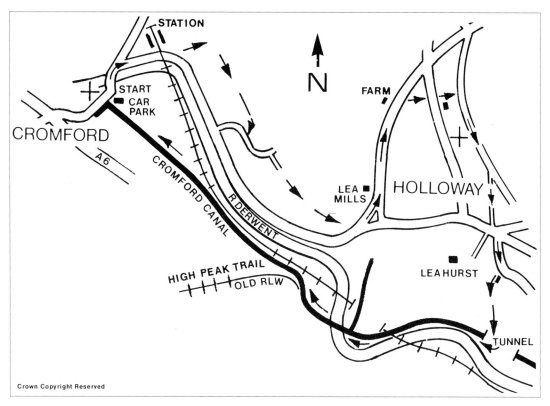

Crown Copyright Reserved

from a lead smelting works now gone, where at one time almost all the lead from the Derbyshire mines was smelted. Opposite a farm, turn right up an enclosed path to a road, crossing it to a path beside a ruined chapel. This emerges in a lane where you turn right past the Lea Rhododendron Gardens (open at specified times). The lane rises steadily, and you may rest by turning through a kissing gate to the Dethick, Lea and Holloway War Memorial, a tall obelisk with a seat set among masses of rhododendrons. With a view far away across the Derwent Valley this must surely be the most beautifully sited memorial in Derbyshire.

Continue up the lane to take a path (right) beside a seat and this drops to a lane and then the main road. Opposite is the entrance to Lea Hurst and you take the road on the left signposted Whatstandwell. On a sharp left bend, cross a stile beside a house on the right and go forward to the corner of the field. Over the stile here, go forward to a green track beneath the trees, and here you are on another drive to Lea Hurst, now seen over on the right. Early one morning in 1856, Florence Nightingale walked up this drive on her return from the horrors of the Crimean War, having caught the early train from London to avoid the publicity and honour the public wished to give her.

Where the drive turns sharp left, bear right past a cottage to continue down a hill ridge with fine views down the valley. Over a stile at the bottom, turn right down to Cromford Canal to find you have just passed over it at Gregory Tunnel. From here back to

Cromford Wharf is an easy and very pleasant three mile walk along the towpath. The canal crosses the railway and then the Derwent at Wigwell Aqueduct where a beam engine originally raised water from the river to maintain the canal level.

Close by is High Peak Junction, the restored wharf where limestone etc. was brought down Sheep Pastures Incline on the High Peak Railway to be transferred to the canal boats. Here is the beginning, or end, of the High Peak Trail which climbs over the lower Peak almost to Buxton.

Near a restored swing bridge which crosses the canal here, a footpath crosses the railway and river to a small car park. This and the Trail adds its quota of walkers, and the return along the towpath to the Cromford car park is very popular, especially at weekends.

On the hills above Holloway

27

No. 13:
Curbar Edge

Route: Curbar Gap – Curbar – Calver – Froggatt – Curbar Edge – Curbar Gap

Distance: 4½ miles

Map: Outdoor Leisure Map O.S. 1:25,000 – The White Peak

Car park: Curbar Gap

There are many exhilarating walks along the gritstone edges in Derbyshire, and non finer than that which runs high above the Derwent Valley at Baslow, Curbar, Froggatt and on to the Derwent Reservoirs. There are serveral car parks and many people are content to walk along the edges and then retrace their steps. This is very rewarding, but it is much more satisfying to follow a circular route, and this one includes a walk beside the river. For the more energetic this can be combined with walk No. 16 as a look at both maps show. This one starts at Curbar Gap and drops down through Curbar to Calver. It then follows the river to Froggatt before climbing steeply to Froggatt Edge. The walk back along the edge to the car park is sheer delight.

Close by the car park at Curbar Gap stands an old guide stone, its lettering now almost obscured, and for centuries this indicated to travellers across the open moors that here was a gap in the gritstone edge.

A number of packhorse tracks converged on the gap, for this was an important trade route in the 15th century and no doubt long before. Your route lies down the road and there are other interesting features often missed; biblical references carved on the huge stones lying around. They were carved by Edwin Gregory who was a mole catcher employed by the Duke of Devonshire. He was also a local preacher and carved these texts in thanksgiving after surviving a serious illness. One is inscribed from Isaiah 1.18 and reads – 'Come now, let us reason together', a text for all ages.

Where a road joins on the right, look for the curious stone built into the wall, and puzzle about its purpose. Near the bottom of the hill a circular pinfold seen on the left is of interest and then you join the old main road in Calver. This portion of road with the church, public house and old bridge were by-passed about 10 years ago. Turn on to the old bridge and look at the gaunt mass of the mill almost hidden by trees. This replaced an older mill and was built in 1805, a 'dark satanic mill' typical of its time. Should it be vaguely familiar, then you may have seen it featured in the *Colditz* series on television.

Go forward from the bridge and turn right between the cottages along the mill road and where this turns right to the mill, go straight on through a gate. The open road passes a farm and an attractive building surmounted by a bell-cote without its bell. This was originally a school built by the mill owner for his apprentices. Beyond the school the road enters trees and runs beside the mill leat to emerge in a road at New Bridge, where you cross over and continue

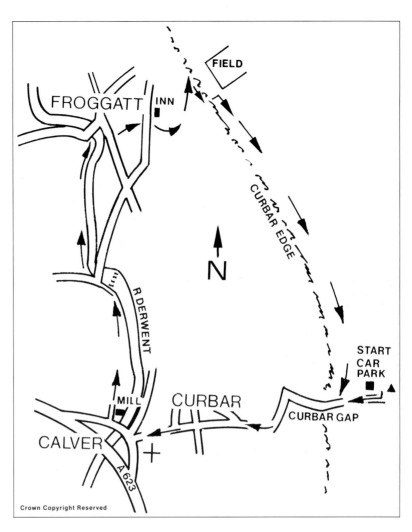

beside the river to Froggatt Bridge. You may, however, wish to turn onto the bridge where, at least half a mile from Calver Mill, is the mill dam, its still waters reflecting the rocky skyline of Curbar Edge, your return route.

Froggatt Bridge has a high pointed arch and a smaller one only one vehicle's width, and this you cross and turn right. In about 100 yards a stile gives access to a river bank path back to Calver Mill if you are daunted by the climb to Froggatt Edge – remember the climb through Curbar village, however! Otherwise continue along the road a short distance to a stile beside a gate on the left and go straight up an open field. When the *Chequers Inn* comes in sight, aim towards a gate and stile about 100 yards to the right of it. Across the road a broad track climbs through the trees, going off right and then curving left to the foot of Froggatt Edge where you climb through the boulders to the top.

The route right to the car is clear; a rough sandy track snaking over the moor some distance from the rocky edge. Even on a warm sunny day it is not difficult to imagine the grim journey it would be over these windswept moors in bad weather, for this rough track was once an important road to Sheffield.

A much more rewarding choice is to follow the edge of the escarpment and enjoy the superb views across the valley. Our outward route in the valley is clearly seen with Middleton Dale beyond. Should it be clear, the village of Stoney Middleton can be seen in the dale, and a little higher up the grey cottages of Eyam cling to the slopes of Sir William Hill. Walk No. 15 crosses this hill from Eyam to Abney. The unfinished millstones lying around are evidence of an industry once practised along these edges.

A geological cross section through the Peak at this point shows these edges as the surfacing of a layer of Millstone Grit, a corresponding layer occurring across the county near the Goyt Valley. In between lies the thick limestone dome of central Derbyshire with its wonderful dales. One wonders at the aeons of time taken to lay these sedimentary rocks down and the slow process of eroding them away. 'A thousand ages . . . are like an evening gone'. In some places one can feel very small and unimportant. Curbar Edge is such a place.

Reform Tower on Stanton Moor

No. 14:
Darley Dale

Route: Darley Bridge car park – Clough Wood – Birchover – Stanton Moor – Stanton Lees – Car park

Distance: 7½ miles

Map: Outdoor Leisure Map O.S. 1:25,000 – The White Peak

Car park: Darley Bridge

The gritstone plateau of Stanton Moor stands high above Darley Dale and is a fascinating area of national archaeological importance. Measuring only two miles long by one mile wide it has prehistoric burial mounds and a stone circle besides other interesting features of more recent date. This walk follows a packhorse track from Darley Bridge to Birchover and then circles Stanton Moor before returning through Stanton Lees.

From the car park near Darley Bridge turn right to cross the river and then right in the village opposite the Post Office. Where the road tops the hill the village of Stanton Lees is seen nestling beneath the slopes of Stanton Moor with the residue of the old Mill Close Lead Mine in the middle distance. This is your return route, for here you turn left, the road deteriorating into a rough track where it enters the trees. The track forks and your route is to the right,

but first you may like to turn left a short distance to see the site of the original Mill Close Mine. An old photograph of 1875 shows this spot as a hive of industry, but all that remains today is the ruined beam-engine house. When the workings extended northwards a new shaft was sunk on the site mentioned previously and when flooding caused it to be abandoned in 1939, underground workings had reached Rowsley nearly a mile away.

Returning to the fork you follow the other track uphill beside a wall; then it bears left and falls steadily to become a green lane. This is an old packhorse track along which lead was carried from the hills to the river crossing at Darley Bridge. The lane improves where it serves a farm and then joins a road at Upper Town, a part of Birchover with only one or two houses – and a set of stocks! A notice records that they were restored by J. C. Heathcote, of a well-known Birchover family who actively, and expertly, excavated the ancient burial mounds on Stanton Moor and whose findings now lie in the museum at Sheffield.

Turn right to the village and then right up to the hill top where you will find extensive remains of quarrying. Here at a junction close by a deep working quarry, a signpost points to Stanton in Peak, your route for about half a mile. Resist the temptation to turn onto the moors until you come to a path marked by a huge block of stone deliberately placed there. Within a short distance a stile gives access to the moor, an area of sandy paths where one can wander at will among the heather.

At a huge monolith called the Cork Stone turn left, to follow the edge of old quarries and pass through

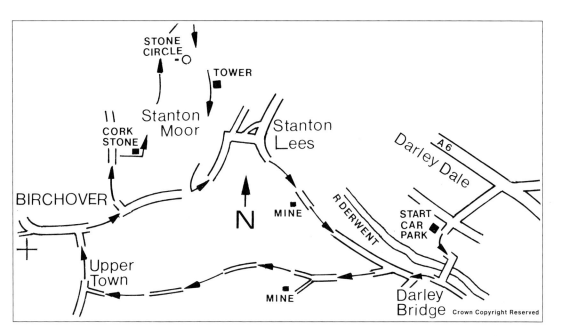

Crown Copyright Reserved

patches of silver birches, and follow a fence right down to a rough track. Here you turn right, and although your route soon leaves the track to turn left down a path to a stile, you may wish to turn right into the trees to find the Nine Ladies Stone Circle. The purpose of this feature in the lives of the Bronze Age people who inhabited this hill top, is not fully understood, nor is that of King Stone a short way away, typical of the isolated stones often found near such circles. A legend of the 19th century tells us that they are maidens and a fiddler turned to stone for dancing on the Sabbath.

Return to the track and cross the stile with the square tower in view ahead. This was built by the Thornhill family as a tribute to Earl Grey who carried the Reform Bill through Parliament. A stone tablet carved with a coronet and 'Earl Grey 1832' which was set above the doorway has unfortunately disappeared in recent years. This is a pleasant vantage point at which to linger, with extensive views across the Derwent Valley. The path continues along the edge of the moor (cross the stile back onto the moor again) passing the Cat Stone, Gorse Stone and Heart Stone with no indication of why they were so named; we should know, however, that we are indebted to Mr. F. A. Holmes MA, JP, of Buxton who presented Stanton Moor Edge to the National Trust.

The path becomes a sunken track which drops to the Birchover-to-Stanton Lees road, where you turn left. Here are distant views of Riber Castle beyond Matlock as you twist and turn steeply down to Stanton Lees where you turn right and right again. The road passes through the old workings of the Mill Close Mine and you soon join the outward route back to the car park.

Remains of original Mill Close Mine

31

No. 15: Eyam

Route: Eyam – Highcliffe – Nether Bretton – Abney – Stoke Ford – Sir William Hill – Eyam

Distance: 6½ miles

Map: Outdoor Leisure Map O.S. 1:25,000 – The White Peak

Car park: Hawkshill Road, Eyam

This is a fairly strenuous walk, but well worth the effort. It climbs over Eyam Edge to cross Bretton Clough to Abney, and then drops down Abney Clough to Stoke Ford. From there it climbs through the heather over Sir William Hill and then drops steeply back into Eyam. The village is, of course, famous for its heroism during the plague of 1665-66, and small notices indicate features connected with it. A typical Peakland village, it has a fine Saxon Cross close by an unusual sundial in the churchyard and stocks on the green before the 17th century hall.

From the car park in Hawkshill Road (note the ruined Bradshaw Hall opposite, which preceded the hall in the village) turn up the road and at a sharp bend, leave it by forking left. In a short distance the road becomes a rough track which climbs and twists steeply to emerge on a road opposite Highcliffe Barns. Turn left and continue over the hill, turning sharp left where a rough road comes down from Sir William Hill on the right. In a short distance turn

right along a rough lane. Where this becomes a good road on a left bend with two cottages, a signpost (Footpath to Abney) stands beside the gateway of the second cottage. Go down beside the house to enter a field over a stile.

Your route passes Cockey Farm seen in the distance, but in between lies Bretton Clough. You cross two fields aiming slightly left to a stile in the corner and then follow the wall to another corner stile. From here a well-worn path twists down into the valley bottom, crosses the brook and climbs to the fields above. Cross a stile and follow a wall on your right over two fields, then aiming to the right of Cockey Farm and its farm road. Here was born William Newton, owner of Cressbrook Mill beside the River Wye, whose child labourers, in contrast to those of Litton Mill just up-river, were kindly treated. Self taught, he was a poet who is remembered as 'Minstrel of the Peak'.

Where the farm road bears left round the farm, go straight ahead to a stile and cross the next field obliquely left to cross a small stream. Turn right along the top of the opposite bank to cross a step-stile. Cross the footbridge seen below and climb to Abney. Turn right on the road and just over a small rise pass through a gate on the right with a sign 'Footpath to Eyam via Stoke Ford 3¼ miles'. This is the farthest point of your walk.

The track can be very muddy for a few hundred yards to a gate, but through this the very pleasant path drops gently down the wooded Abney Clough to Stoke Ford. Here the Bretton and Abney Brooks

Opposite: Path down Abney Clough

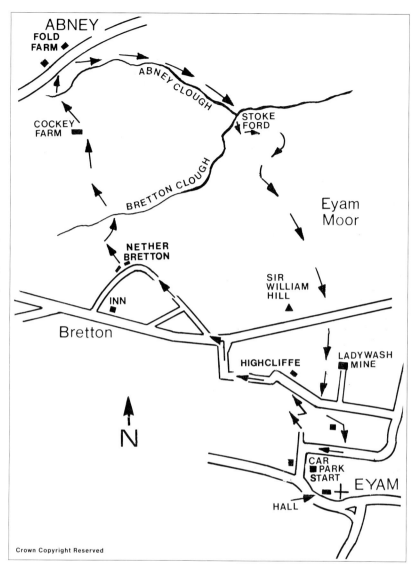

ABNEY
FOLD FARM
ABNEY CLOUGH
STOKE FORD
COCKEY FARM
BRETTON CLOUGH
Eyam Moor
NETHER BRETTON
SIR WILLIAM HILL
INN
Bretton
LADYWASH MINE
HIGHCLIFFE
N
CAR PARK START
EYAM
HALL

Crown Copyright Reserved

join and several very ancient tracks cross. Tradition has it that it was to this deep wooded clough that the people of Eyam drove their cattle for safety when Bonnie Prince Charlie retreated from Derby in his invasion of 1745. Whether true or not, one could easily hide numerous cattle in this lonely spot.

Cross the two footbridges and note that your route to Eyam is indicated by one of those old cast-iron signs erected by the Peak District and Northern Counties Preservation Society, that early pioneer of ramblers' rights. Where the path forks at the top of the bank you keep right. This path continues up Bretton Clough but within a few yards you leave it to turn sharp left up a sunken track. This is the Eyam route which climbs steadily as it bears right round the hillside, giving extensive views down to the Derwent Valley and the rocky edges above Hathersage. The path turns back towards Bretton Clough, becoming roughly enclosed as it runs along its edge. Where the path forks into three, left and right following the walls, you go straight ahead towards the hilltop along a worn path defined by posts and set in the heather. Here you are on Eyam Moor and from the hilltop Sir William Hill is seen over on the right crowned by a mast. Here nearly 1,500 above the sea, there are extensive views across the Derwent Valley to the east and the hills to the north.

The worn path is seen twisting through the heather about midway between the mast and the buildings of the Ladywash Lead Mine on the left,

and soon strikes a rough road. This is wide and straight and was once an important turnpike road to Buxton. Called Sir William Road, it was probably named after Sir William Savile, Lord of the Manor of Eyam in the 17th century. From the stile opposite, the path once passed through the workings of the old Ladywash Lead Mine seen over on the left, but has now been re-routed to go straight ahead beside the wall to join the road.

Cross the stile on the opposite side of the road and cross the field obliquely left towards the corner of a wood. Follow the wood side to the corner, pass through the stile and turn right down the wood side to a path which drops steeply down through the trees to a road. On the right the fine Youth Hostel stands among the trees and across the road a sign indicates two footpaths to Eyam seen far below. Your shorter route, however, is to the right down the road, soon bringing you to the car park.

No. 16:
Froggatt Edge

Route: Hay Wood car park – Froggatt Edge – Froggatt – Grindleford Bridge – Hay Wood car park

Distance: 5½ miles

Map: Outdoor Leisure Map O.S. 1:25,000 – The White Peak

Car park: Hay Wood

This walk along Froggatt Edge and beside the River Derwent can be combined with Walk No. 13 as mentioned there. The steep rough track between the edge and Froggatt village in the valley below is thus avoided in this combined walk. From the car park at Hay Wood it crosses the B6054 road and goes along Froggatt Edge to the point where it connects with Walk No. 13 and then drops down to Froggatt village. From there it crosses the fields to Grindleford Bridge and then climbs steadily on smooth paths through delightful birch woods back to the car park. In the woods there are bluebells and wood anemones (and those large brown wood ants!) all in season of course.

Leaving the car park at Hay Wood at the opposite end to the entrance, cross the steep little gorge and brook to the road. Turn right a short distance and cross it to pass through a kissing gate onto Froggatt Edge. Not far away on the right is a rocky outcrop with distant views far up the Derwent Valley. The houses of Nether Padley shelter among the trees covering the steep slopes dropping to the river and Grindleford Bridge. The sandy track winds through silver birches some distance from the edge, with occasional rocky viewpoints across the valley. The rough track crosses a brook, one of the hazards when this was an important road into Sheffield, and after crossing the stile here, look for a small stone circle amongst the heather on the left. Hardly noticeable now, this ring of stones is nevertheless significant to the experts, who tell us that these moors were once peopled by Bronze Age folk. One can only conjecture what purpose these circles served so long ago.

The track now runs close to the edge with extensive views across the valley to Sir William Hill, its lower slopes scarred by Stokehall Quarry. After passing between huge rocks you make contact with Walk No. 13, and here you leave the edge. From here you drop down to Froggatt village, this portion being walked in reverse in No. 13. Those who made this walk will remember the way up through the edge, otherwise the way down is not too obvious and you proceed as follows: an enclosed field on the left is your guide (as shown on the map) and you continue to the end of it and then turn off the edge in a dip.

Opposite: dramatic views from Froggatt Edge

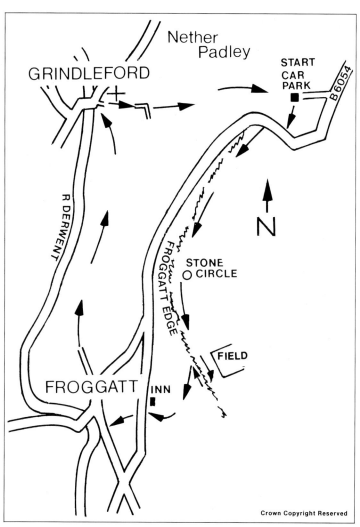

GRINDLEFORD

Nether Padley

START CAR PARK

B6054

R DERWENT

N

FROGGATT EDGE

STONE O CIRCLE

FIELD

FROGGATT | INN

Crown Copyright Reserved

Below: Path through Grindleford Woods

Here a smooth path doubles back below the edge and it reaches its lowest point at the foot of the rocky face. Several large domed millstones lie around, and here you turn down a steep rocky path into the wood.

The path twists down to a road with the *Chequers Inn* a short distance away. Cross the road to a stile and go straight down the field to join the road in Froggatt. Turn right to the graceful 17th century bridge but do not cross, going forward along a raised pavement past pleasant cottages. Where this ends cross the road to enter a lane, noting the garden wall made of vertical stones around Rose Cottage.

The lane becomes a footpath which crosses the fields, passes through National Trust woods and emerges at Grindleford Bridge. This is an old turnpike road as evidenced by the attractive toll house seen across the road. Your way lies up the rough road on the right, and where this bends right you leave it by going straight ahead into the wood. You follow the wall on your left, a stream tumbling between the rocks in a 'Welsh Fairy Glen' on the right.

Where the wall ends continue straight up through the trees, and where a wider path leads off right go straight on up a narrow path. The huge rocky crag on Froggatt Edge, mentioned at the start of the walk, comes in sight high on the right. Soon you join a wide path where you turn right, and crossing a stile, enter Hay Wood and the car park.

35

No. 17: Goyt Valley

Route: Goyt's Lane car park – Errwood Reservoir – Wildmoorstone Brook – Cromford and High Peak railway – Car park

Distance: 3 miles

Map: Outdoor Leisure Map O.S. 1:25,000 – The White Peak

Car park: Goyt's Lane

This short walk takes you into one of the most beautiful corners of Derbyshire, the Goyt Valley. Unlike Walk No. 18 in the lower part of the valley, this one visits the moors on the eastern side of the Errwood Reservoir. From the moors it drops to the reservoir beneath which once stood the little hamlet of Goyt Bridge. It then climbs for about one mile (a Derbyshire mile = about one and a half miles!) beside Wildmoorstone Brook and returns along the route of the old Cromford and High Peak Railway.

The pool beside the car park is formed by the embankment which carried the railway and you cross this route by going down Goyt's Lane and turning through a gate beside the pool. The cutting through which the road curves is the line of the railway and also the steep incline beyond, which drops to the reservoir embankment. This was

Bunsal Incline which was worked by a steam engine here, but nothing remains today.

Through the gate you turn right along a level track, in a short distance turning left down a green lane. This is a continuation of the road beside the car park, its lower end now cut by the flooding of Goyt Bridge. This pleasant grass-covered lane was open to cars until the reservoir came in 1967; now it is known only to walkers. Thus only the walker will know the delightful spot where the twisting road turns into the waters. Here is a grassy knoll with fine views.

Across the water the distant moors are cut by the wooded defile of Shooters Clough running down to the waters edge. Here was the entrance to the drive, shrouded with rhododendrons, which ran up to Errwood Hall, the ruins of which can still be visited. The bridge seen there carries a diverted road across this arm of the reservoir and can be reached by continuing from the car park down Bunsal Incline and crossing the reservoir embankment. Immediately below you another short arm runs up Wildmoorstone Brook and here once stood a tiny 17th century packhorse bridge. It stood on a saltway from the Cheshire salt mines and today this historic bridge can be seen higher up the Goyt Valley where it has been re-erected across the river by Stockport Water Board who built the dam.

Today not even the name Goyt Bridge appears on the map to remind us that here once stood this bridge, another which carried Goyt's Lane across the

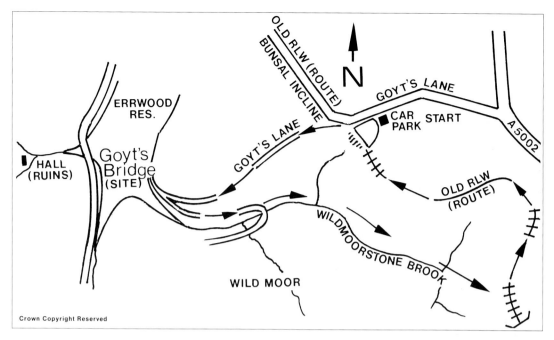

Crown Copyright Reserved

river, this area now being all submerged. At this spot a rough track turns sharp left, and you turn your back on the scene and follow it along the high slopes of Wildmoorstone Brook valley with Wild Moor seen ahead. The track drops to the brook which is crossed by two huge steel girders, incongruous in this lonely moorland setting. Here you leave the track by keeping to the left of the brook and climb to the head of the valley and the embankment of the Cromford and High Peak Railway. This path, like so many beside streams on the moors, can be wet in places.

On the embankment a view to the right shows Burbage Tunnel which passes beneath Burbage Edge, a watershed, for the waters which drain from its eastern slopes drain into the North Sea, and those here into the Irish Sea. This portion of the railway opened in 1831 and ran for 61 years, so your route back to the car has remained undisturbed since 1892. It is easy and level, following the contour lines except for embankments and low cuttings and known only to walkers and sheep, giving extensive views across the Goyt Valley.

Opposite: Wild Moor

Right: the Errwood reservoir

No. 18: Goyt Valley

Route: Fernilee Reservoir – Mill Clough – Taxal Village – Goyt Valley – Fernilee Reservoir

Distance: 4¼ miles

Map: Outdoor Leisure Map O.S. 1:25,000 – The White Peak

Car park: Fernilee Reservoir

The lower end of the Goyt Valley is still deep, wooded and secluded, unlike the upper parts which have become so popular that traffic congestion occurs in the summer months. The centre portion has been transformed by two reservoirs, the Errwood and Fernilee, which are also very popular and there are a number of car parks in the area. Although there were several cars in the Fernilee park, we did not meet any other walkers in this lower end of the valley, and this walk crosses the reservoir embankment and then Mill Clough before running along the slopes of Taxal Edge. It then drops down to the tiny village of Taxal and returns in the depths of the Goyt Valley.

My old Ordnance map, used long before the reservoirs came, shows that the car park stands on the route of the Cromford and High Peak Railway, this portion of which opened in 1831 and closed nearly a century ago. From the car park, cross the embankment and look up towards the Errwood Reservoir. This was once wooded like the view downriver and beneath the waters of the reservoir lie the remains of a gunpowder mill which were covered when the valley was flooded in 1937.

Turn right and soon a left bend reveals Mill Clough, too steep to cross straight over, so the road drops obliquely down the side to climb out in a sharp bend up the other side. In the clough bottom a small ruined building beside the stream houses the remains of a pump which no doubt once pumped water to a farm above. Halfway up the hillside the now green road passes through a gate and climbs to a sharp bend near Overton Hall Farm which stands on the site of the old hall.

Just before reaching the farm you may rest on a seat by courtesy of the Whaley Bridge Amenity Society and enjoy extensive views. High on the right the upper reaches of Mill Clough are clothed by Goyt Forest while across the Goyt Valley lies the village of Fernilee with the gabled hall prominent among the trees. The rough, open road climbs past the farm to join the good road which here ends at a locked gate into Goyt Forest. Turn right along the road which runs along the slopes of Taxal Edge with bilberries and rhododendrons on the open hillside. Soon Sitch House is passed, its curious name explained by its situation in a dip in the hillside. 'Sitch' occurs frequently in Derbyshire and means a spring or small watercourse.

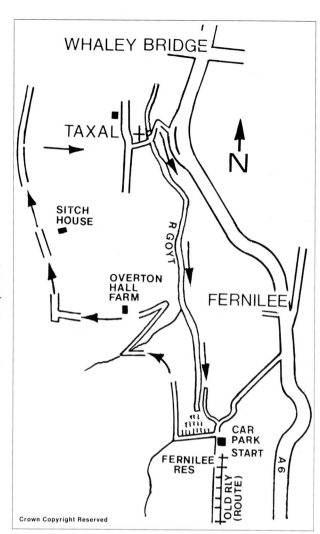

Crown Copyright Reserved

Below: a corner of Taxal Village

As you pass a narrow wood on the left, look for a step-stile opposite. From here a distant view includes parts of Whaley Bridge below on the left and the blue line of Kinderscout on the skyline. Drop straight down the open field to a stile and follow the footpath beside the wall to Taxal. Where the path joins the road you turn left past the attractive white vicarage to the church. Your way runs down the rough road beside the church but first you may wish to go forward to the 17th century inn, *The Chimes*.

Look in the church if possible where a tablet to Michael Heathcote records that he held the dubious office of 'Gentleman of the Pantry and Yeoman of the Mouth to his late Majesty King George the Second'. No doubt a well-fed post but not without its dangers. Taxal is an ancient place, its name coming from Saxon times, and a chapel has stood here since at least the 13th century when the very powerful Lords of the Manor lived at Overton Hall mentioned earlier.

Had you taken this walk 50 years ago you would have been in Cheshire, for before 1936 the River Goyt was the county boundary, and you now drop down to the river by going down the churchyard – noting the arched tomb of 1706 – and emerging in the rough track already mentioned. This is an ancient saltway running from the Cheshire salt mines to Sheffield and beyond. It drops steeply to the river and ford (footbridge) and climbs equally steeply up the other side; there seems no doubt that this old river crossing has changed little for centuries.

Where the track bends sharp right you go through a small gate into Shallcross Wood also on the right. The path runs along the hillside before leaving the trees and dropping down to the flat fields beside the river. Here there are no features, just solitude and pleasant walking, and I was set to wondering why the Ordnance Survey cartographers had thought it necessary to change Dale of Goyt on my old map to Goyt Valley today.

The path eventually becomes a narrow road which passes through the yard of the water-works below the embankment before climbing back to the car park.

39

No. 19:
Great Hucklow

Route: Great Hucklow – Windmill – Little Hucklow – Hazelbadge Hall – Quarters Farm – Great Hucklow

Distance: 4½ miles

Map: Outdoor Leisure Map O.S. 1:25,000 – The White Peak

Great and Litte Hucklow are two delightful Peak villages about three miles north of Tideswell and situated at the head of a green valley which develops into the limestone gorge of Bradwell Dale. This walk crosses the fields by way of the little hamlets of Windmill and Little Hucklow down to the beginnings of Bradwell Dale at Hazelbadge Hall. It returns along the slopes of Durham and Hucklow Edges which dominate this side of the valley and, like so many such hillsides, can be very wet through surface water draining down.

Great Hucklow has a broad main street and you leave it by passing the Queen Anne public house at the west end, the road soon becoming unenclosed. Here a long view down the valley includes the twin peaks of Lose Hill and Win Hill flanking the entrance to Edale in the distance, while the top of the tall chimney of the cement works at Hope showing over the hills cannot be ignored. The disrupted

surface around us is evidence of a much older industry, the workings of a surface vein of lead, or 'rake'. This continues through Windmill seen ahead, but there is no evidence of the windmill which gave the hamlet its name.

You turn right at crossroads and then right again down the main road. After passing a barn on your left you cross a stile to follow the wall, bearing right across several fields, two of which are very narrow as they curve over the hill – curious. Joining a rough track, you follow it to cross a shallow valley and go straight along a narrow field. Little Hucklow comes in sight and crossing a stile on the left you continue beside the wall to the road. Turn left to village.

The *Old Bull's Head* is an interesting pub, for its walls are adorned with ancient farm implements and leadmining tools while all around are old ploughs etc. together with two huge cheese presses. Do not miss the Hall of 1661 behind the pub. At the second bend you leave the road to follow an enclosed path beside the last farm building on the right. Where this ends continue down the field to a corner where a stile gives access to another enclosed path. This joins a road where you turn right to Lower Farm seen ahead. Here you turn left in front of the house to a stile on the right.

Following the wall on your right you cross a stile, and from here your route crosses the fields in the direction of Bradwell Dale, with good step-stiles all the way. This is sheep country and when we were there in March the hills were alive with ewes and their lambs, almost every one with twins. Each stile had been heightened by wooden bars to deter these agile animals. In Green Dale you cross a stile and

Opposite: path into Little Hucklow

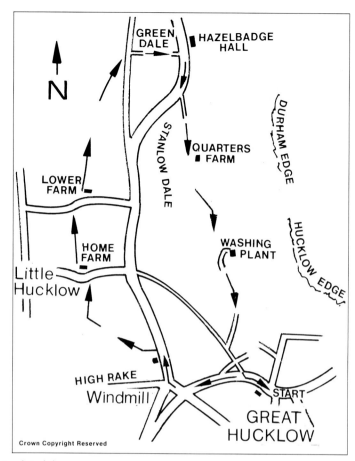

Crown Copyright Reserved

*Below: Hazelbadge Hall dating from
1549 with its mullioned windows*

minor road and go down an enclosed track to join a
main road. A short distance away on the left stands
Hazelbadge Hall of 1549, with the coat of arms of the
Vernons to whom it once belonged. A grim legend
tells of how a member of the family, Margaret, rode
down the dale to Hope to see the man she loved
married to another. Crazy with misery, she rode
home to die and on dark stormy nights you may see
her ghost galloping frenziedly through this rocky
gorge, back to Hazelbadge Hall.

Turning up the main road you leave it at the first
bend by turning left along a rough lane. This goes
only to Quarters Farm where you cross a stile to the
right of a farm building. Here you climb to a gateway,
follow the wall on your left to another, and then turn
left up an open field to a stile in the far top corner.
The path follows the wall on your left to the corner,
but a little detour away from the wall may be
necessary to avoid surface water draining from the
'edge' above mentioned earlier.

Through the stile you bear left to join a rough road
which serves a washing plant. From these slopes
Windmill is seen high on the hill and Little Hucklow
nestling in its hollow. The two curious parallel fields
referred to earlier are very noticeable. The way back
to Hucklow is straight forward, the road joining
another where a left turn brings you to the outward
route in the village.

41

No. 20: Hartington

Route: Hartington – Pilsbury – Pilsbury Castle – Hartington

Distance: 4½ miles

Map: Outdoor Leisure Map O.S. 1:25,000 – The White Peak

Car park: Near Hartington Market Place

The village of Hartington in the Dove Valley is famous for its cheese. To the TV viewer and *Coronation Street* addict it had brief fame as the mythical retirement home of Hilda Ogden. To the rambler, however, it is the northern end of the seven mile long footpath beside the River Dove through the beautiful limestone gorge comprising Dovedale, Milldale, Wolfscote Dale and Beresford Dale. North of Hartington the valley is less well known with more gentle terrain through Pilsbury until it reaches the dramatic peaks of Parkhouse and Chrome Hill and on to the Dove's birth on Axe Edge.

This walk follows the river to Pilsbury and the site of its castle, and although along a road, this is unenclosed and gated and very little used by vehicles. It can, however, be very muddy in wet weather. The

return is an exhilarating footpath walk along the hillsides with extensive views up and down the valley.

From the Market Place go past the village pond, soon leaving the cottages and then passing Bank Top Farm. When Ludwell Farm comes in sight, look for a lead mine adit close by a gate across the road. Beyond the farm, originally a corn mill, a large spring emerges from beneath the road at the next gate. Although a 'Lud Well' is shown on the map hereabouts, this has all the appearance of a sough cut to 'unwater' the lead mines situated on the hills above.

In Pilsbury, just two farms pleasantly set among trees, the road makes a zig-zag climb to leave the valley. This is an old pack-horse track which crossed the Dove here on its way between Leek and Bakewell and the enclosed route can be seen dropping in a straight line down the Staffordshire hills across the valley. On a sharp right bend in Pilsbury you leave the road and go straight on down a rough farm track.

Soon the impressive mounds of Pilsbury Castle come in sight. Although on private land, a stile gives access and close by a metal plate records its scant history together with a fine line drawing showing how it is thought to have looked. The motte and bailey are still clearly discernible after over 900 years, for we read that it was built in 1068-69 by William the Conqueror to repel raiders from the north. Early man had inhabited these hills long before

Opposite: site of Pilsbury Castle

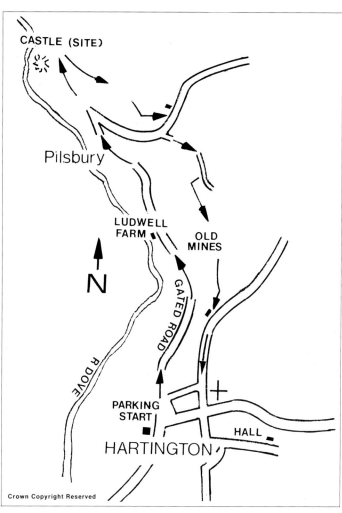

CASTLE (SITE)

Pilsbury

LUDWELL
FARM

OLD
MINES

↑
N

GATED ROAD

R DOVE

PARKING
START

HALL

HARTINGTON

Crown Copyright Reserved

*Below: the village of Hartington with
its village pump*

the Conqueror came, for the maps show a tumulus on Pilsbury Castle Hills and these you now climb by turning sharp right up a steep path. Here a backward look gives a fine view up the valley with the sharp peak of Parkhouse Hill prominent among the jumble of hills reaching back to Axe Edge on the skyline. Near the hilltop a notice informs you that the footpath has been diverted, the path now continuing beside the wall. Over the next stile you rejoin the old path by crossing two fields, and emerging on a road to the right of a barn.

Here you deliberately deviate from the green dotted line on the Ordnance Map which runs up the field across the road. Instead you turn right to the bend in the road and then leave it to turn left along a farm track. Crossing a stile beside a gate you turn right beside the wall and where the farm track turns left towards a derelict farm you turn right through a stile continuing beside the wall now on your left.

Over a stile, you climb a well-worn path from which you see stiles below where you pass between hummocks from the lead mines mentioned earlier. Cross the next open field to a gap, follow the open hillside and then aim down to the corner of a walled field. With the wall on your left you cross a farm track and then leave the wall side and pass through three stiles, aiming towards a new farm on the hill. A stile beside the farm buildings on the left gives access to the road which drops pleasantly back into Hartington, turning right at the church to the Market Place.

No. 21:
Hathersage Moor

Route: Fox House – Burbage Moor – Hathersage Moor – Fox House

Distance: 6 miles

Map: Landranger Series O.S. Sheet No. 110

Car parking: Beside the road near Fox House

This walk straddles the border with Yorkshire on the high moors above Hathersage. Unlike the walk over the lonely hills above Hayfield (No. 22) this one is well used on summer week-ends. This is largely due to the nearness of Sheffield which is seen in the distance at one point, and there is little doubt that the hard gritstone so abundant here played a part in its growth as a steel city. There is still evidence of this in the form of unfinished millstones and troughs. Again remember there is no shelter on the moors, but the route is dry and very pleasant.

You can park beside the A625 road between Toads Mouth Rock and the *Fox House Inn* which lie

on the Sheffield road about two miles out of Hathersage. Follow the road round the inn, and it was here, lovers of 'Jane Eyre' may like to know, that Jane left the coach to walk the lonely miles to 'Moor Seats', the North Lees just north of Hathersage on your map. The Eyre family was large in those days; Charlotte Brontë knew Hathersage well and there are a number of 'Jane Eyre' associations in this area.

Continue towards Sheffield and in about a quarter of a mile, where the road bears right, take a rough track straight ahead. The track undulates for about two miles over Burbage Moor with Sheffield seen far below on the right, and where it crosses a stream there are scant remains of habitation, an old milestone indicating that this was once a main route into the city. In the next dip you fork left up a track which soon runs beside a pine plantation and the Ox Stones come into view over on the left. A path leads to the stones where you bear right through the heather to a stile seen ahead with a South Yorkshire sign beside the road.

Turn left along a pleasant verge path beside the road, with wide views across Hallam Moor, a sea of cotton grass in season. The road dips to Burbage Bridge where a magnificent view is seen down the valley of Burbage Brook with Higger Tor and Carl

44

Opposite: the Ox Stones on Burbage Moor

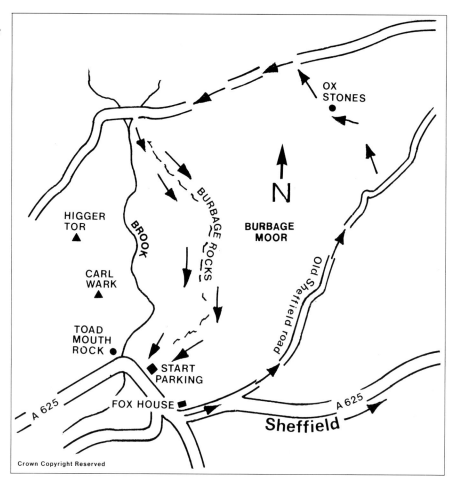

OX STONES

N

HIGGER TOR ▲

BROOK

BURBAGE ROCKS

BURBAGE MOOR

Old Sheffield road

CARL WARK ▲

TOAD MOUTH ROCK ●

◆ START PARKING

A 625

FOX HOUSE ■

A 625

Sheffield

Crown Copyright Reserved

Below: an old trough on the moor

Wark on the right and Burbage Rocks on the left. Here you have a choice. Either take the easy smooth green track down the valley beneath the rocky edge or the route along the windy edge itself with its panoramic views. From this you can drop down to the lower path at several places as you approach the main road and car parking.

This peaceful valley of rocks and heather looks as though it has always been so, but soon you may notice evidence of the hand of man among the heather in the form of huge stone troughs and mills-tones showing that here there must have been a thriving industry. Old records show that whole familes worked and lived here, fashioning the huge rough blocks of stone with hammer and chisel, a hard life in bad weather on this exposed moor. 'Peak' millstones were renowned, and one wonders at the problem of transporting these heavy items into Sheffield and to remote mills and farmyards.

Of much older history is the fort of Carl Wark seen across the valley, but the experts are not entirely sure if it is Iron Age or dating from after the Roman occupation. This high defensive site has been strengthened with a rough wall of stones 10 feet high and 100 feet long with an earth ramp. Various paths

lead to it, an obvious one running from a stile beside the main road near Toads Mouth Rock, and it makes an easy and very pleasant short walk.

45

No. 22: Hayfield

**Route: Hayfield – Sett Trail – Birch Vale – Moor
Lodge – Throstle Bank – Ridge Top – Hayfield**

Distance: 7½ miles, 5½ miles and 3½ miles

**Map: Outdoor Leisure Map O.S.
1:25,000 – The Dark Peak**

Car park: Hayfield Station (set trail)

Hayfield, a pleasant textile village nestling among
the hills east of Kinder Scout, is the start of this walk
which climbs 800 feet to follow old tracks across the
hilltops. Very often these tracks across the northern
hills – one time farm roads, bridle roads or packhorse
tracks – have been worn into 'hollow ways', gullies
which become brooks in wet weather. Thus one
needs to be particularly well shod, and remember
there is no shelter on these lonely hills. There are no
unusual or remarkable features on this walk, just
solitude and wide panoramas.

The railway along the valley of the River Sett
between Hayfield and New Mills closed in 1970 after
running for 102 years. It was acquired by the
Derbyshire County Council in 1973 and became the
Sett Trail, the station site at Hayfield now a picnic
site with the usual facilities. Although 7½ miles long,
this walk is not too strenuous, and a look at the map

shows shorter versions of 5½ and 3½ miles marked
with an 'X'.

From the picnic site go along the trail, crossing a
lane on the way, to where a footpath crosses the trail
at a large mill dam. Here you turn left off the trail up a
short path to a main road junction. Cross over and
follow the main road right and leave it by forking left
opposite a chapel. The wide road climbs steadily,
serving a huge quarry before becoming a rough track
along the hillside. Over on the right New Mills fills
the valley, and soon beyond this, if the air is clear, you
may see the high rise flats of Stockport in the
distance.

Just before the attractive white buildings of Moor
Lodge are reached a stile on the left is the route for
the shortest walk already mentioned, meeting the
return route near a mast. For the longer walks,
continue along the rough track to where a good road
joins on the right, with rough open ground opposite.
Should you wish to take the 5½ mile walk, turn left
beside the wall to a walled track (signpost – Bridle
Road). This runs for several hundred yards as a
sunken track, and in wet weather can be difficult with
rocks and mud. Beyond this the way is pleasant to
the skyline where the track of the long return route
crosses.

To take the full walk continue forward with
extensive views opening up towards Whaley Bridge
in the valley below. Where the track joins a smooth
lane at a sharp bend, turn left along the lane into a

Opposite: one of the wide panoramic views to be enjoyed on this walk

Below: Moor Lodge

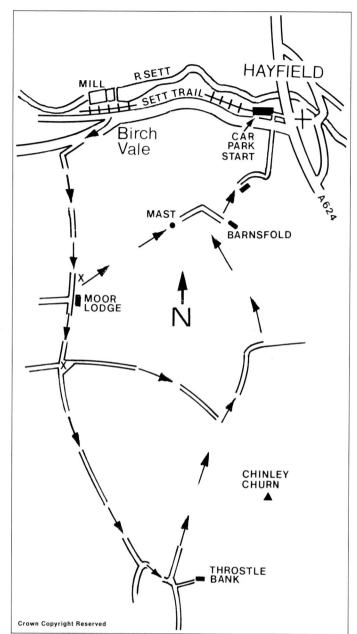

Crown Copyright Reserved

dip. The buildings seen ahead are Throstle Bank. Here you leave the lane by turning left up a rough sunken track and enter the National Park, having walked along the edge of the Park all the way from Moor Lodge. The track climbs the side of Chinley Churn and continues to the point where the 5½ mile walk joins on the left. The track becomes enclosed by high walls and after a sharp right bend, you are on open moorland (signpost).

This is the highest point of the walk. In the distance the skyline is the edge of Kinder Scout, with the well-known William Clough climbing to a dip on the horizon to the left. A little to the right of this a smaller dip indicates Kinder Downfall where the River Kinder falls sheer from Kinder Edge. In very windy weather, after heavy rain, the water is swept back in a great plume of spray, seen even at this distance of four miles. Here you turn left beside a wall, the well-worn path leading down towards Hayfield partly hidden in the valley. Beyond the village can be seen the main road climbing past Little Hayfield on its way to Glossop over the hill. The curiously shaped peak to the left is Lantern Pike, a National Trust property.

It is all pleasantly downhill now, the open track curving left towards the right of the mast mentioned previously. Soon it runs beside a wall to enter a road through a small gate, the meeting point with the shortest walk. Turn right down the road to a gate and cross the stile beside it. Follow the wall down the field on the left, cross the stile in the corner and turn right up a farm road to pass through a farmyard. Here is a lane which twists a little before going straight down to the picnic site in Hayfield.

The High Peak trail seen from Black Rocks at Cromford

No. 23: Middleton by Wirksworth

Route: Middleton Top car park – Cromford Black Rocks – Sheep Pastures Incline – Cromford – Via Gellia – Middleton by Wirksworth – car park

Distance: 5½ miles

Map: Outdoor Leisure Map O.S. 1:25,000 – The White Peak

Car park: Middleton Top (High Peak Trail)

A wealth of industrial archaeology set in fine scenery is the reward of this walk. From Middleton Top on the High Peak Trail near Wirksworth it follows the trail past Cromford Black Rocks to Sheep Pastures Incline. From there it drops to Cromford, passes through the woods of the Via Gellia and climbs to Middleton by Wirksworth and thence to the car park.

The engine still works at specified times at Middleton Top, but the cable pulleys used for lowering the waggons down the steep incline here are now still, for the line closed in 1963. This is one of a number of inclines needed on this railway, for it crossed the hills of central Derbyshire to link the Cromford Canal with the Peak Forest Canal at Whaley Bridge. It was built in 1825-31, being opened in stages.

From the engine house descend the 1 in 8½ incline and where it levels off it is hard to imagine that just over 25 years ago this now overgrown area was a very busy junction where sidings served the Middle Peak Quarry. Soon the trail runs along a high stone embankment with extensive views down the Ecclesbourne Valley and with Wirksworth seen in the distance. The intermediate area of old quarries is now England's first stone museum, called the National Stone Centre which can be visited en route. The trail passes at the foot of the Cromford Black

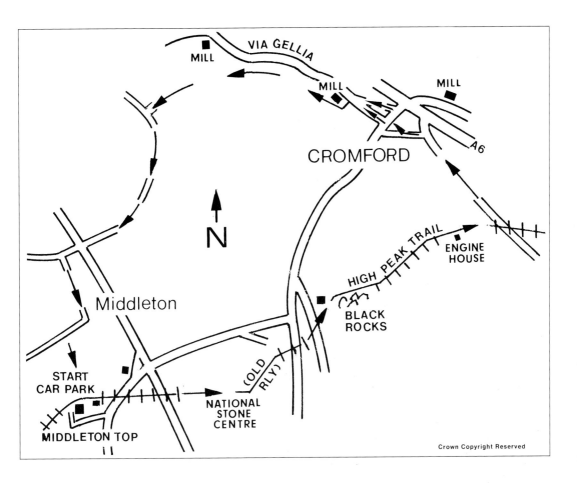

Crown Copyright Reserved

Rocks seen ahead (car park) and soon fine views are seen up the Derwent Valley with Cromford far below and Riber Castle high on its hilltop.

The next feature is the engine house, now a mere shell, with its attendant derelict water supply at the top of Sheep Pastures Incline. This has a drop of 1 in 9 straight down to Cromford Canal but you leave it to join a rough road which passes beneath. This is easily reached by leaving the trail a short distance before the bridge, turning right to a quarry track. Here you turn under the bridge, the road becomes a good surface where it serves new bungalows, and you go down towards the main A6 road.

In sight of the main road turn left through a wide gateway and go forward to emerge in North Street. Cromford is Sir Richard Arkwright's village and the street is flanked by three-storied mill houses, the top floors being workshops, while the end of the street is blocked by the school he built. Retrace your steps a few yards and pass through a stile in the wall. The path passes behind cottages and here is a deep hole where the Cromford Sough emerges, draining the lead mines around Wirksworth. It disappears, finally appearing again to cross Mill Lane by a cast iron aqueduct and enters Cromford Mill.

The path comes out on Cromford Hill and you turn down to the Market Place. In 1790 Arkwright

secured a Market Charter, having built the *Greyhound Inn* 12 years previously. Here you could turn left along Water Lane but may prefer to cross the Market Place and turn up the narrow lane called the Scarthin. This runs above the mill dam past the *Boat Inn* before dropping to Water Lane. Cross over into a short road, pass through a stile and then almost immediately on your right, entering the Via Gellia woods. The pool below powered the old corn mill close by, together with a paint grinding mill a few yards down Water Lane.

The well-worn path through the trees is pleasant, and where it strikes the edge of the wood you turn left beside the wall to a stile. Cross this and follow the wall left round the edge of the field and re-enter the wood by another stile. The path climbs steeply and emerges from the wood to become an enclosed track for a short distance before climbing to an enclosed farm road. Here you turn left to Middleton Village where you pass Mount Zion Chapel and cross the main road. Soon you turn left into The Moors (sign on the wall) and a very pleasant track climbs between derelict quarries with extensive views across to Riber Castle. The track, now enclosed, reaches Middleton Moor and you leave it by crossing a stile on the left. From here an open track crosses the fields and soon the engine house at Middleton Top comes in sight.

No. 24:
Monsal Dale

Route: Taddington Dale car park – Brushfield Hough – Upperdale – Cressbrook Mill – Monsal Trail – Monsal Dale – Taddington Dale car park

Distance: 5 miles

Map: Outdoor Leisure Map O.S. 1:25,000 – The White Peak

Car Park: Bottom of Taddington Dale

The increasing number of car parks in the countryside testifies to the continuing popularity of rambling. 50 years ago there were comparatively few cars on the roads, walkers using the bus services and railways, and older readers may remember the 10.20 ramblers' train to Buxton being already full when it drew into Derby Station from Nottingham. Old and young disgorged at each station and were not seen again until re-boarding the train, and even in the popular dales one met only the occasional walker.

This reminiscence came to mind in the car park at the bottom of Taddington Dale where there is easy access to the very popular Monsal Dale. This walk, however, climbs high onto the hills above the dale and drops down to Upperdale beside the Wye to go on to Cressbrook Mill. The return is by the Monsal Trail and an easy walk beside the river back to the car.

From the car park beside the A6 at the bottom of Taddington Dale you cross the road to a stile into Monsal Dale. The path drops to stepping stones and a stile over which you leave the dale by turning left. (Signpost). The path twists and climbs steeply through trees and hawthorns and where it emerges into the open there is a fine view down the Wye Valley with Great Shacklow Wood on the right.

Here you veer right to cross a stile and join an open road. Turn right towards Brushfield Hough, a farm standing on the edge of Monsal Dale which here falls steeply and gives a clue to the farm's name. The little hamlet of Brushfield lies across the fields to the left; according to Ekwall's book of place names, 'Hough' means 'spur of the hill'. Just before the farm you turn left through a gate into the farmyard, turn left round a building and leave by another gate into an enclosed road. (This is where those little yellow arrows, which are becoming so numerous, are so useful).

50

Opposite: the viaduct in Monsal Dale

*Did this walk 20.6.01.
Our own version of it
as beginning part of path
through woods to Brushfield
closed due to Foot & Mouth
epidemic. Dry and windy
then Sunny. Lovely walk.
Lovely day.*

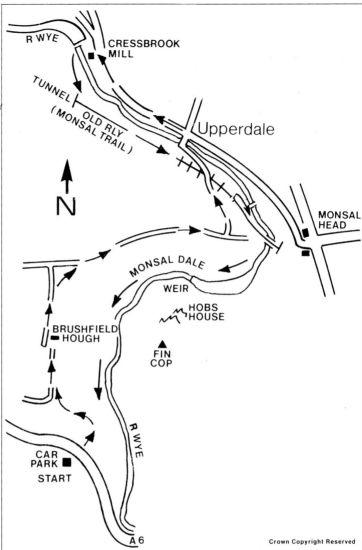

Turn right and where the road enters the second field note the hillocks of a lead 'rake' left and right. Here you aim across towards the top corner of the field on the right to turn right along a road. This runs along the edge of Monsal Dale with fine views, the weir on the river shining white far below. Across the dale Fin Cop stands high, a perfect site for the Iron Age fort which stood there, and down its smooth slopes juts a rocky outcrop. Maps show this as Hobs House, a common name often relating to the Hob Goblins of more superstitious days.

Soon the Monsal Head Hotel comes into view across the dale and after passing a deep lead 'rake' you turn left at a junction and drop down to Upperdale. Here you have passed beneath the old railway, now the Monsal Trail, and as this is your return route you could shorten the walk if desired. At Upperdale, cross the river and turn left along the road to Cressbrook Mill. Turn through the gateway and yard to the mill dam. The mill itself, more attractive than some large houses, is not the first on the site and once used child labour, the children being housed in Apprentices Row close by.

Turn left across the dam wall to a footbridge over the river and climb a path which turns left along the hillside. Here you are on the Monsal Trail, joining the old railway route at a blocked tunnel. The line was opened in 1863 and closed in 1968, and it is hard to believe, as one passes through the remains of Monsal Dale Station, that this now overgrown track carried express trains just over 20 years ago.

Where a footbridge crosses the track, you join the footpath and descend to the banks of the Wye near the railway viaduct. From here the path runs down Monsal Dale back to the car park, but one cannot leave this impressive structure without recalling John Ruskin's outburst when the viaduct was being built in 1861. His scathing remark that 'now every fool in Bakewell can be in Buxton in half an hour and every fool in Buxton in Bakewell' is well known. Not so well known, however, is the interesting early reference to the new photography with which he begins his criticism. It should be mentioned that at that time photographic prints could only be produced by exposure to the sun, the result being in sepia. The reference, abridged, is worth quoting –

'You think it a great triumph to make the sun draw brown landscapes for you. That was also a discovery and some day may be needful. But the sun had drawn landscapes before for you, not in brown but in . . . . . all imaginable colours. Not one of you cares for the loss of them now when you have shut the sun out with smoke, so that he can draw nothing more, except brown blots through a hole in a box.'

One wonders what John Ruskin would think of the part photography, with its superb colour, plays in our life today?

51

No. 25: Monyash

Route: Monyash – One Ash Grange – Cales Dale – Lathkill Dale – Haddon Grove – Monyash

Distance: 5½ miles

Map: Outdoor Leisure Map O.S. 1:25,000 – The White Peak

Parking: Beside A5055 outside Monyash

Monyash is a pleasant limestone village with a church founded in the 12th century and old and new crosses on a green overlooked by an old inn. On the A5055 Bakewell road just outside the village, a dip indicates the beginnings of Lathkill Dale and here is parking room for a few cars. The five mile walk down the dale to Alport is very popular and each end of the dale, being so accessible, can be rather crowded on summer week-ends. This walk, however, crosses the hills from Monyash, drops into the dale lower down by way of Cales Dale, and follows the river downstream before returning over the fields to the car.

From the car park follow the road into Monyash.

At the churchyard gate the green can be seen ahead and, should you wish to see the village, continue forward and turn left at the crossroads. Otherwise, turn into the churchyard and leave by the opposite gate. Inside the church are parts of the original 12th century building and a 10 feet long chest thought to be only a century younger. The south porch with its unusual oak tracery is believed to be 19th century. From the south gateway go forward to the main road and turn left. On a right bend go straight ahead on a narrow field lane, keeping left at a fork, to its end at a gate.

Cross a stile to follow the wall on your right and then cross it to drop into Fern Dale. This narrow dry dale was the route of a packhorse track which here dropped into Lathkill Dale and then climbed to Over Haddon and Bakewell. Crossing Fern Dale, the path follows the wall side through stiles, first one side then the other, to a gate across a farm road. Go through the gate and turn down the road to One Ash Grange Farm. As the name implies, this was once an outlying farm belonging to an abbey, although little remains of the buildings which were once a penitentiary for unruly monks of Roche Abbey near Rotherham.

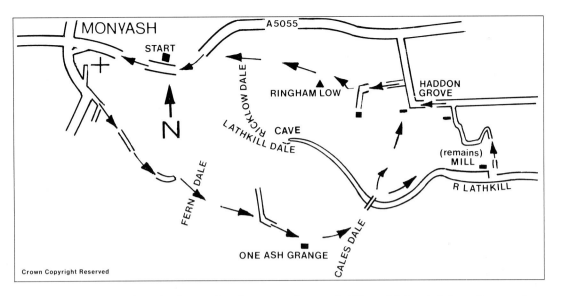

Crown Copyright Reserved

Go through the gate into the farmyard and turn left, passing old pigsties and an underground room perhaps once used for cold storage. The track, which can be muddy in wet weather, drops down the side of Cales Dale to a footbridge over the River Lathkill. Here, of course, you may turn up the dale back to the car. Or you may wish to take the steep path seen straight ahead to pass through the towering limestone cliffs above. Here you would then cross two fields, a narrow wood and the farmyard at Haddon Grove to emerge on the road there, the meeting point with the full walk.

To follow the full walk, turn down the dale to a mill pool. Of Carter's Mill which stood there little remains except two millstones beside the weir and the foundations of the small building built in the early 18th century. Nearly 50 years ago I took several photographs of the mill, then roofless but with its large waterwheel intact and collapsed grindstones inside. The waterwheel was removed for scrap during the 2nd World War. This isolated dale saw other activities in days gone by, for sheep washing took place just above the pool and also at the footbridge we crossed. Higher up the dale there was great activity at Ricklow Quarry, while below the mill there is much evidence of lead mining. Today the dale is quiet, much of it a nature reserve, and peopled only by walkers.

Here you leave the dale by turning left up a green track down which the corn came, and as it twists and climbs steeply one can imagine the horses straining with waggons heavy with flour. At the top the track passes a farm to join a road where you turn left to Haddon Grove. Here, on a sharp corner, is the meeting point with the alternative route. Leave the road by going through the first gate on the left onto a farm track. Where this bends left to a farm continue forward to a stile (signpost). Here you climb a field obliquely right and cross several fields to the right of the trees surrounding Ringham Low. Your route is slightly right of the spire of Monyash Church now seen in the distance and you pause at an open gateway. The Ordnance Map shows the path following a wall here but this has now completely disappeared and you cross the open field. Below lies Ricklow Dale which you cross to climb to a stile indicated by posts in the wall on the far side. Another stile in the left corner of the field ahead leads to a gateway and stile into the road, where a left turn takes you back to the car.

Opposite: view in Lathkill Dale

Right: Carter's Mill some fifty years ago

No. 26: Over Haddon

Route: Over Haddon – Youlgreave – Bradford Dale – Alport – Over Haddon

Distance: 4½ miles

Map: Outdoor Leisure Map O.S. 1:25,000 – The White Peak

Car park: Over Haddon

The lower reaches of the River Lathkill and its junction with the River Bradford form one of the loveliest areas in Derbyshire, and as it is so easily reached and there are several parking spots, it is also one of the most popular. This portion of the path in Lathkill Dale can be almost overcrowded on summer weekends. This walk, however, crosses the Lathkill and goes over the hills to Youlgreave, drops into Bradford Dale and on to Alport. It returns over the hills to Over Haddon, thus avoiding any crowds beside the Lathkill.

From the attractively terraced car park at Over

Haddon, take the twisting road down into Lathkill Dale. The clear waters of the river can be non-existent in very dry weather but one should cross the ancient clapper bridge of limestone slabs to see the myriad of sea shells revealed by the polishing of countless feet. The path zig-zags up the wooded slopes to emerge in an open field. Your way lies through the farmyard of Meadow Place Grange, which as its name implies was a farming outpost of some distant abbey and once had its own chapel, of course.

Cross the farmyard and pass between farm buildings to emerge in the field (signpost), and following the wall on your left, climb two fields to a road. Turn right a few yards to a signpost opposite indicating Youlgreave. The village is seen in the distance and your path crosses a shallow valley towards the left of a small clump of fir trees. Here you join a rough track which goes on to a road into the village, entering it at Old Hall Farm. Here the road forks and you have a choice; whether to visit the church – very rewarding – or drop straight down into Bradford Dale.

To visit the church, take the left fork and join the main road at The Fountain, the fanciful name given to the huge water tank there. Note the equally fanciful Tom Thumb Hall close by! Turn left to the

Opposite: in Bradford Dale

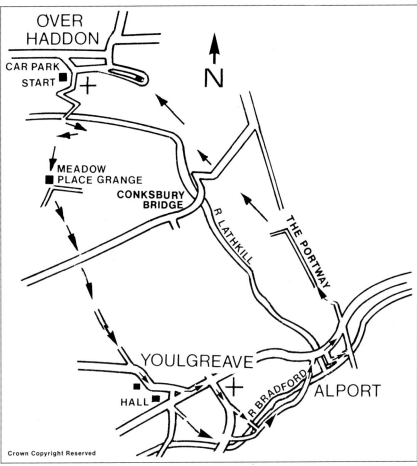

OVER HADDON

CAR PARK
START

MEADOW
PLACE GRANGE

CONKSBURY
BRIDGE

R LATHKILL

THE PORTWAY

N

YOULGREAVE

HALL

R BRADFORD

ALPORT

Crown Copyright Reserved

church and see the Norman font, for there is not another like it in England. Turn right at the church and at a right bend take a narrow track left down to a delightful packhorse bridge, the meeting point with the alternative route.

For this alternative route, fork right at the Old Hall Farm to cross the main road to the school, noting the charming Old Hall of 1656, built 26 years after Old Hall Farm. Your way turns left beside the school and enters a path at the end of the road to descend steeply to the River Bradford. The river is soon crossed by a clapper bridge and by a road bridge too, also made of stone slabs. Continue beside the river to the packhorse bridge and the meeting point with the alternative route.

Continue along the road beside the river where low limestone cliffs add greatly to its charm, noting the covered lead mine shaft, one of many in this area. The main road is joined at Alport where the Lathkill meets the Bradford, and you cross the Lathkill to leave the main road by turning down right between the cottages. Here is another bridge with a weir and ancient cornmill. A lovely spot and the reason for this diversion, for here you turn left back up to the main road which is crossed to a rough lane. From the bridge you have been on the prehistoric route known as the Portway which crossed Derbyshire from the

south east to the north west.

Climbing the rough lane, the valley of the Bradford opens up, now thickly wooded. Yet in the middle of the last century it was bare of trees and the site of a large lead smelting works, a photograph of that time showing large buildings, chimneys and flues cut into the hillside. Some years ago with permission, for the ground is private, I explored these workings for the foundations are still there, all completely overgrown and hidden, yet another portion of Derbyshire's industrial archaeology.

The lane bears left at farm buildings and the Portway can be seen continuing straight on as a green track between stone walls, heading for the hills west of Bakewell to cross the River Wye at Ashford-in-the-Water. You follow the road left to find a stile on the right. Across the fields can be seen Over Haddon and the footpath aims straight towards the white building of the Lathkill Hotel in the distance. Cross two fields to a road, once the main road between Bakewell and Ashbourne which crosses the Lathkill over Conksbury Bridge down to the left. From the stile opposite cross the next field and continue along the edge of Lathkill Dale, leaving this and heading straight for the hotel where a stile leads into the road. The way back to the car park is straight through this very attractive hilltop village.

No. 27: Taddington

Route: Taddington – Chelmorton – Churn Hole – The River Wye – Blackwell – Taddington

Distance: 6½ miles

Map: Outdoor Leisure Map O.S. 1:25,000 – The White Peak

Taddington is one of the hill villages of the Peak, standing astride the old A6 high above the Wye Valley. Since a new by-pass was built some years ago this pleasant village is no longer plagued with traffic and thus a safe place to start this walk. This takes you even higher over Taddington Moor with fine panoramic views over the White Peak. The church has a stone reading desk, not common in

Derbyshire, and six feet of an ancient cross in the churchyard which defies the experts to say if it is Saxon or Norman. It should be mentioned that there is a very steep and rocky descent into Churn Hole. A look at the map shows an alternative route but this too is down a steep but grassy hillside.

Leave the churchyard by the top gate and cross the road to a stile and an enclosed path. Climb two small fields obliquely right to a road. Cross the stile opposite and follow a lightly defined path towards gaps seen in the wall up ahead to the right. Aim towards the left of a flat-topped hill (an underground reservoir) seen ahead when a stile will be found at its base.

Here you are nearly 1,500 feet above sea level on the great limestone dome of central Derbyshire. Down below to the north the River Wye has cut its gorge to the Derwent and beyond, the dark gritstone mass of Kinder Scout dominates the skyline. To the

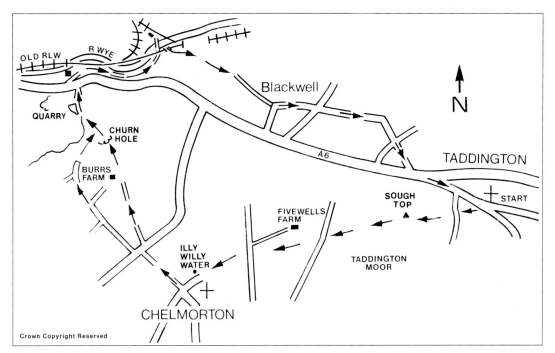

Crown Copyright Reserved

south the undulating hills are enmeshed in a lacework of white walls. I took a piece of limestone and examined the sea shells which were laid down at the bottom of the sea millions of years ago, and remembered how well Lord Tennyson describes the impermanence of these seemingly solid hills.

> *'There rolls the deep where grew the tree,*
> *O earth, what changes hast thou seen!*
> *There where the long street roars has been*
> *The stillness of the central sea.*
>
> *The hills are shadows, and they flow*
> *From form to form, and nothing stands:*
> *They melt like mist, the solid lands*
> *Like clouds they shape themselves and go.'*

The stiles continue through the fields heading to the left of Five Wells Farm seen ahead and you cross a green lane, pass one field away from the farm to emerge on a farm road. Cross over, slightly right, and continue down the rough workings of a lead-mining rake to emerge behind the church in Chelmorton. Over a stile on the right is a spring with the quaint name Illy Willy Water which runs down the shallow valley in which the village lies, and was no doubt the reason for its existence. The church has the highest situation in Derbyshire and is of Norman origin with a large selection of carved stones in the porch.

Turn down the village street and just before a junction on the left, turn right along a minor road to cross a cattle grid. This is Coals Lane, along which came coal from the mines near Buxton. Where the lane joins a road, two farm roads are seen opposite, slightly left and right, and here are the alternatives mentioned earlier. The right one passes close by Burrs Farm, the path dropping down a shallow valley

to Churn Hole set among trees. Here the path twists steeply down the rocks into a dark gorge with a small cave, and one can imagine the waters churning and forming this hole long ago. The path continues down the dale to emerge on the A6 road by way of the Topley Pike Quarry entrance. To miss the difficult descent into Churn Hole you take the left road. This leads over the hills and where it ends you cross a field obliquely right to the corner and drop steeply down the hillside to join the path below Churn Hole and on to the A6 road and the car park opposite.

Pass through the car park and follow the rough lane beside the Wye to a footbridge over the river. Here is a row of cottages, with evidence of a mill which once stood here, and here is the junction of Great Rocks Dale, the most quarried dale in the county although those at this bottom end are now disused. The view downstream from the bridge shows one of our loveliest limestone gorges, Chee Dale, the route of Walk No. 10, where a footpath runs beside the river to Millers Dale. Today, however, you retrace your steps about 50 yards and climb the short distance to the old railway, now the Monsal Trail. From the bridge, look at the deep cutting eastwards towards Monsal Dale and Bakewell and westwards to the end of the Trail a short distance away.

Cross the bridge, bear left along a green track for about 100 yards and cross a stile. The worn path zig-zags steeply up the rocks to continue beside a field wall to the right. It then crosses two fields diagonally left and aims to the top left corner of a field to enter a farm lane over a stile beside a gate. The lane joins a road into Blackwell where you go straight on into the village and cross two crossroads before joining the Taddington by-pass. Cross over to go down the old A6 back into the village.

The River Manifold at Ilam

No. 28: Thorpe

Route: Thorpe – Coldwall Bridge – Ilam – Dovedale – Lin Dale – Thorpe

Distance: 6 miles

Map: Outdoor Leisure Map O.S. 1:25,000 – The White Peak

Car parks: Thorpe (Ilam Hall and Dovedale)

This walk crosses the border to Ilam in Staffordshire and returns by the stepping stones in Dovedale. The Ilam Estate is now a country park and this beautiful area is very popular, especially at summer week-ends. No excuse is made for this walk, however, for it should be remembered that there are always new people moving into the county and also young folk walking it for the first time. The outward route to Ilam is not so well-known and may make a change for some who do not know the area as well as they perhaps think. (Note that there are car parks at Ilam Hall and Dovedale, should the small park at Thorpe be full.)

From the car park in Thorpe cross the road and go on to the church which has a typical Norman tower. The excellent church guidebook tells us that the tall sundial in the churchyard may have been made for horse riders and thus moved here from another site.

This seem to be born out by the fact that the style is set at 53° exactly whereas the latitude at Thorpe is 53°03″. These three seconds, angle seconds and not time seconds, could make quite a difference in position and one cannot imagine the famous clock makers Whitehurst of Derby who made it, making such a mistake.

Leaving the churchyard, continue down the road which passes through a gateway and becomes a track which twists down into the Dove Valley. It is, therefore, a surprise to find a milepost in the valley bottom which reads 'Cheadle 11', and even more surprising to find the road crosses the river on a long impressive bridge. This is Coldwall Bridge, built in 1762 to carry this once important road linking the Blythe Marsh turnpike in Staffordshire with the Ashbourne-Buxton road. One cannot help wondering if the sundial in the churchyard on the hill had a connection with this ancient highway.

Cross the bridge, which incidentally was originally only half the width, and note there is no indication of the road on this Staffordshire side of the river. Passing through a stile on the right you follow the hedge on the right and enter the riverside meadows over a fence stile. Turn left to reach the river where the Manifold merges with the Dove and continue along the bank to the road bridge at Ilam. Turn over the bridge and then left past the Eleanor-type cross, taking the path left to the church just before the hall drive.

There is far more at Ilam than can be mentioned

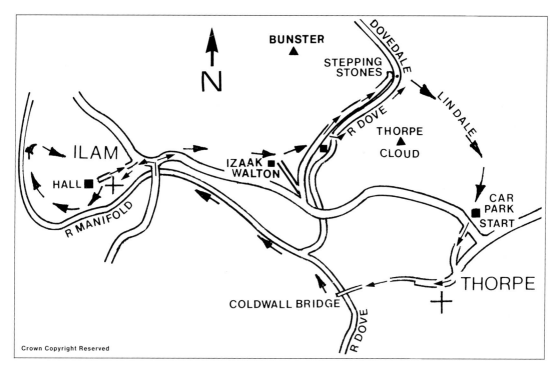

Crown Copyright Reserved

here, but look at the two Saxon crosses in the churchyard, the Saxon font, and the paper garlands hanging high in an arch, a relic of the old custom of carrying them at the funeral of a virgin. Close by is the simple tomb of the founder, St. Bertram, where miracle cures for the afflicted were said to take place. In contrast is a wonderful full-size group sculpture by Sir Francis Chantrey of the Watts-Russell family who built the Hall and the cross near the bridge, and also transformed the village as you see it today.

Leave the churchyard by the gate facing the hall and turn left down to St. Bertram's Bridge, passing a spring also named after the Saint. Turn up river to a low cliff where the rivers Manifold and Hamps surge up from their underground courses close together, yet they have completely separate routes below ground. This is proved by the fact that there is always a few degrees difference in temperature between them, although Dr. Johnson refused to believe it when he visited Ilam with Boswell. Here the Doctor wrote 'Rasselas', and you may like to climb a path nearby to an alcove above, where William Congreve wrote 'The Old Bachelor'.

The path continues beside a low wall where the river curves in a great amphitheatre of woods in a spot called Paradise. Where the path crosses the river, you turn away from it up a track to the right which leads to the hall, and here you pass through an arch to the front. Today it is a youth hostel, which, together with the 50 acres around, is the property of the National Trust, a gift from Sir Robert McDougall. There is a shop here and teas.

Leave the hall grounds by the drive and pass the cross. Beyond the last cottage garden go through a small gate to bear right up a worn path to a cart track.

Go through a stile beside a gate and aim across the field to the left of farm buildings where three hedges meet. Here is a stile and you go forward to pass the *Izaak Walton Hotel*, bear left to the car park below, and emerge in the road into Dovedale. Turn left to a footbridge over the river and here you have a choice.

You may continue along the road to cross the stepping stones, which can be tricky sometimes, or cross the bridge and go along the other bank to the same spot, where you turn up Lin Dale. If you feel very active, cross the bridge and climb Thorpe Cloud to drop down into Lin Dale. From the top the views are extensive with Ilam Hall down to the west and Dovedale to the north, most of what you see being National Trust property, much of it also the gift of Sir Robert McDougall. The footpath up Lin Dale runs into a track which leads back to the car park at Thorpe.

The tomb of St. Bertram in Ilam Church

Water-cum-Jolly Dale

Opposite below: the way through Litton Mill

No. 29: Tideswell Dale

Route: Tideswell Dale Picnic Site – Litton Mill – Water-cum-Jolly – Cressbrook Mill (alternative Litton Mill – Cressbrook) – Litton – Tideswell Dale Picnic Site

Distance: 5 miles

Map: Outdoor Leisure Map O.S. 1:25,000 – The White Peak

Car park: Tideswell Dale Picnic Site (charge)

One of the loveliest stretches of the Wye Valley is the gorge popularly known as Water-cum-Jolly, although the name does not appear on the Ordnance Maps. It is only one mile long and flat easy walking but not as well used as might be, perhaps because people are doubtful of passing through the mill yards of Litton and Cressbrook at either end. Although the rough road is private, there is a concession for walkers. Should you already know the dale there is an alternative route where the dale is seen from above. From the picnic site in Tideswell Dale, this walk drops into Millers Dale, goes from Litton Mill to Cressbrook by either of the alternative routes before climbing over the hills to Litton and back to the picnic site.

The path at the bottom end of the picnic site leads down to the road and river in Millers Dale, where you turn left to Litton Mill. The few cottages overlook the mill dam, and the mill buildings fit tightly between the limestone cliffs, a pleasant peaceful scene. Yet this lovely spot experienced a sad period in our history in the early 1800s when very young children comprised the labour at the mill under terrible conditions, also common in other parts of England. The whole sorry tale is told by a crippled survivor in his pamphlet 'The Memoirs of Robert Blincoe'.

Here at the mill gates you decide which route you prefer: to continue down the dale to Cressbrook Mill through Water-cum-Jolly, or to go over the hill to Cressbrook Village as shown on the map here. Firstly the dale route.

This is part of the Monsal Trail and you pass through the mill yard to follow a wide track beside the river. The river soon becomes a large pool, reflecting the sheer white cliffs of the gorge when the dam itself is reached at Cresswell Mill. Here is a curious church-like building attached to a row of cottages called Apprentice Row where the children employed at the mill were housed. Unlike those at Litton, these were well treated. The mill itself is an attractive building of 1815 with a lantern on the roof, but there were mill buildings on the site long before this. Pass through the gateway and turn left up the road, keeping right at a fork and continuing to a

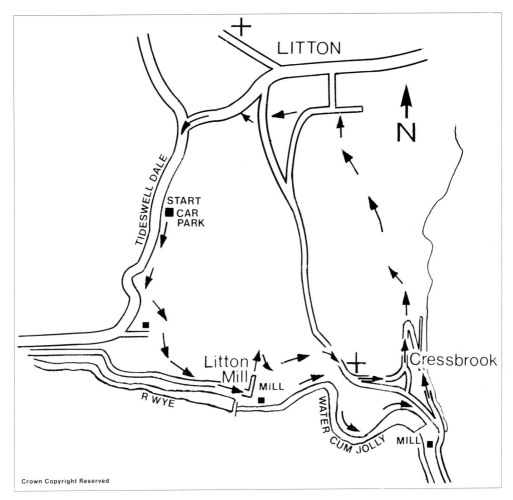

Crown Copyright Reserved

sharp left hairpin bend. This is the meeting point with the alternative route.

Back at Litton Mill gateway, for the other route follow the road left between old cottages with curious round chimneys. The road becomes a track and enters a field to continue up a shallow valley. In a short distance turn right up a track which cuts back sharply to zig-zag up the valley side. The round chimney seen over on the right served an underground flue from the mill. The rough road climbs steadily to emerge in a road with Cressbrook church seen on the right. The gorge of the River Wye is now far below, and after passing the church the view into the dale is magnificent as you proceed down into Cressbrook village. Where the road forks keep left, soon entering the woods in Cressbrook Dale and continuing downhill to the sharp hairpin bend where the alternative route joins.

From the bend a rough track enters the trees, and just before it enters an open field a path climbs the hill on the left (signpost Litton 1 mile) emerging in open fields on the hilltop. In the distance can be seen the village of Litton, and stiles will be found in line with it, crossing the fields obliquely as the path drops into the shallow head of Tansley Dale. From here it climbs a narrow field to a road at a field road junction.

Turn left, and where the road bends left go through a stile ahead, follow the wall for three small fields and cross the fourth field obliquely left when signposts will be seen ahead. Cross the road and stile keeping to the right of the wall to drop to a stile on the road below. Turn left, then left at the junction and back to the picnic site.

61

No. 30: Tissington

Route: Tissington Trail car park – Fenny Bentley – Tissington Trail – Tissington car park

Distance: 4 miles

Map: Outdoor Leisure Map O.S. 1:25,000 – The White Peak

Car park: Tissington Station (Tissington Trail)

The old axiom 'It's an ill wind that blows nobody any good' is still true today. When the 'Beeching axe' fell on our railways in the early 1960s it created new amenities for the rambler in the form of new footpaths. Stations became car parks and picnic areas and the not so able walker can now enjoy level walks through cuttings and over embankments, giving new viewpoints not previously seen. For the more active walker these 'trails' along the old railway routes, linking up with older existing footpaths, have created many new circular walks. This one starts from the old station at Tissington and crosses the

fields to Fenny Bentley. From there it climbs over the hill to the Tissington Trail and thus back to the car park.

From the station turn right on the road and cross the bridge and in a short distance a signpost indicates a footpath across the fields on the right. Passing through a gateway you cross the field diagonally to a stile in the far corner. Follow the hedge on your right and emerge in the lane to Basset Wood Farm on the right, ignoring a lane which forks left. In April the farm has a lovely mass of daffodils bordering the lane.

Leave the lane by crossing a stile on the left opposite the farm and cross the field to a gateway and then follow the hedge on your right, the village of Fenny Bentley coming into sight as you descend into the valley of Bentley Brook. Where you cross a footbridge into an open field you aim slightly right to pass the corners of two fields, turning right at the second to a stile beside a gate and enter a lane. This crosses a brook and emerges on the main road.

Close by on the left stands one of Derbyshire's most charming manor houses, with what looks like a

*Opposite: the village of Tissington and
its pond*

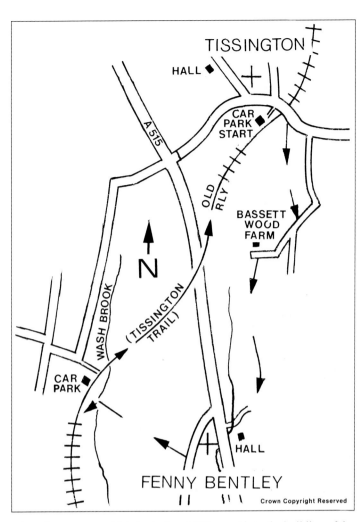

Below: Fenny Bentley Hall

fortified tower remaining from the previous house. This was the home of the Beresfords and one must certainly look at the tomb of John Beresford in the church across the road where he and his wife are shown tied up in shrouds and completely hidden. This, it is thought, is because the sculptor had no reference to their apperance as the tomb was erected nearly a century after their deaths in the 15th century. Unfortunately the figures of their 21 children, also in shrouds, which adorn the sides of the tomb are hidden by pews. Other interesting features too numerous to mention here, can be found with the aid of an information board provided.

Leave the churchyard by the top gate and turn left. Cross a stile beside the last house on the right and climb over the hill through several stiles. The deep little valley of Wash Brook comes into sight and you cross by a footbridge seen below and climb slightly left up a rather wet hillside to join the Tissington Trail. Turning right you pass a car park and picnic area, formerly a station which served the area around Thorpe. The easy 1½ miles return to Tissington car park passes over high embankments and through deep cuttings which show the hard hand labour which in the late 1900s went into the building of the railway which ran for only 65 years.

63

No. 31: Wormhill

Route: Wormhill – Millers Dale – Monks Dale – Wormhill

Distance: 4½ miles

Map: Outdoor Leisure Map O.S. 1:25,000 The White Peak

Wormhill stands high on the hills above Millers Dale, an attractive little village completely belying its name. From there this walk drops down to the River Wye and follows it to the village of Millers Dale, climbs up Monks Dale (with an alternative) and returns over the hills to Wormhill. It should be mentioned that the top end of Monks Dale through the Nature Reserve is wooded and overgrown with the path very rocky and steep in places. An alternative runs along the hill tops to drop to the head of the valley to join with the original route.

From the church in Wormhill turn to the road through the village and turn left. Over the wall are glimpses of the fine hall of 1697, and just round a bend you turn right down a track beside a bungalow. This develops as a rough path along the edge of a deepening dale, and where the path turns away

follow the dale in a short deviation to see a fine view of Chee Dale. This portion of the walk from the church was covered in reverse in Walk No. 10 which came down Chee Dale seen far below. The path continues down to the River Wye and a footbridge but you follow the river downstream. This is the Monsal Trail and you may climb to the old railway bridge to follow it to Millers Dale station and village. Your path, however, follows the river, very pleasant, and emerges in the village where you cross a road and go on to the church. Here you turn up an enclosed path beside the church and emerge in a field where the path forks. The right one drops down into Monks Dale and the route through the dale is unmistakable, passing through an open dale with limestone cliffs in its lower reaches which become hidden by woods as it narrows towards its head. This is the Nature Reserve with its very rough path previously mentioned and readers may prefer the alternative route as follows.

Continuing past the church you fork left beside a row of cottages, and in about 100 yards turn sharp left up a rough track (signpost) to Monksdale Farm. Cross the farmyard to a stile, cross this and turn left behind the farmhouse, joining a rough track (your route) which comes down from the hills. Here you are high above the dale, and on this picturesque spot